You Will Putt Better, I Guarantee It!

You Will Putt Better, I Guarantee It!

by

A. Craig Fisher, Ph.D.

To order additional copies of this book, contact:
Xlibris LLC
1-888-795-4274
www.Xlibris.com
Orders@Xlibris.com
552703

CONTENTS

Acknowledgments 9

Introduction 11

One. Putting Is Not Fair 17

Two. The Harsh Realities Of Putting 23

Three. Factors That Impact Putting Success 33

    Condition of Greens.......................................33
    Green Reading 34
    Distance Control 34
    Accuracy of Irons...35
    Pre-putt Routine and Ritual 35
    Putting Competence/Confidence 35
    Visualization 36
    Self-talking..37
    Emotional Control..38
    Recent Putting Outcomes...............................38
    Outside Factors..39
    Learning vs. Performance Issues 40

Four. Putting Really Is Brain Science................................42

    Strategies to Bias the Image-of-Achievement................48
      The quality of the sensory information....................49
      Your mental approach, attitude, and emotion...........49
      The degree of automatization of your approach 50
      The content and quality of your imagery.................51
      The nature of your self-talking.............................51

Recognize and filter "noise" 52

To Putt Consciously or Nonconsciously,
That is the Question 53

Five. **The Mystery Of Reading Greens**............................**59**

The Process of Reading Greens 62
Reading breaks...63
Reading grain...68
Reading speed...69

Basic Principles, Truths, and Rules of Putting.............77

Six. **Danger Lurks On The Short Grass** **79**

Putting Slumps...79
Missed Short Putts 83
Consistently Missed Putts 86
Good and Bad Putting Days.................................90
What Do You Trust? 93
Excessive Three Putting.......................................94
Putting Yips 95
Failure to Transfer Putting Practice to the Course 99

Seven. **Quest For Competence And Confidence**.....................**102**

Putting Confidence 105
Putting Confidence Drill.......................................109

Eight. **Concentration** **113**

Nine. **Commitment**..**118**

Ten. **Control** **128**

Imagery 128
Role of Imagery in Creating Performance.............129
Characteristics of Imagery 131

Imagery Strategies and Drills.............................133

Thoughts and Emotions 140
   Situations that Require Control............................141
   Strategies to Control Thoughts............................145
   Post-putting Routine 149
   Strategies to Quell Emotions 157

Eleven.   **Consistency**...**164**

Twelve. **Brief Summary**..**168**

   Recognition of Nonconfident Putting...........................168
   Key Principles...170

Ten Commandments Of Putting.......................................**173**

Epilog **175**

References...**177**

ACKNOWLEDGMENTS

Because I do not profess to be the last word on what contributes to putting success nor what undermines success, I have been aided immeasurably by the addition of selected material from others whose permission has been granted to reprint their work in this book. Some names you will undoubtedly recognize (e.g., Dave Pelz) and others will be obscure to you (e.g., Karl Pribram). Credit is most thankfully given to those publishers and authors listed below who deemed this current work worthy of their inclusion.

Excerpt from *The Feeling of What Happens: Body and Emotion in the Making of Consciousness* by Antonio Damasio. Copyright 1999 by Antonio Damasio. Reprinted by permission of Houghton Mifflin Harcourt Publishing Company. All rights reserved.

Excerpt from *Golf My Way* by Jack Nicklaus. Copyright 1974 & 2005 by Jack Nicklaus. Copyright renewed 2002 by Jack Nicklaus. Reprinted by permission of Simon & Schuster Publishing Group. All rights reserved.

Excerpts from *Putting Out of Your Mind* by Dr. Bob Rotella. Copyright 2001 by Robert J. Rotella. Reprinted by permission of Simon & Schuster Publishing Group. All rights reserved.

Excerpt from *Golf and the Spirit* by M. Scott Peck. Copyright 1999 by M. Scott Peck, M.D. Reprint judged to fall under the realm of fair use by Random House. All rights reserved.

Excerpt from *The Art of Putting: The Revolutionary Feel-Based System for Improving Your Score* by Stan Utley. Copyright 2006 by Stan Utley. Reprint judged to fall under the realm of fair use by Penguin Group (USA). All rights reserved.

INTRODUCTION

As I began to plan this book, I read what most others had written about putting. At the same time I regularly questioned my capabilities of telling golfers how they could improve their putting. I often caught myself asking whether I could package the information in a way that would resonate with golfers of all abilities. I certainly didn't want this book to be an academic exercise nor, heaven forbid, did I want to be accused of adding any more confusion to the whole encyclopedia of golf instruction. I've heard it said many times that the best way to ruin your golf game is to read whatever new is being published monthly in the golf magazines: *Thy this . . . Try that.* I wanted this book to contain enough "meat" so that every golfer who reads it will find several means of improving their putting, thereby reducing their handicaps. It is to this end that every day spent writing this book had your best interests at heart, and no day went by without reminding myself to present the very best case I could. I know we all can putt better, but I also know that changes will of necessity have to be made. Do we seem to play better day after day, week after week, month after month, and year after year? Or, do we epitomize Albert Einstein's definition of insanity: *Doing the same thing over and over and expecting different results*? It is my promise to you that this book will offer you hope and solutions for a better golfing future.

I've written this book in what I call conversational style because I want to talk with you, ask you questions, pique your curiosity, prick your conscience, even have you argue with me when you think I'm off base. I've had many decades of golfing experience and years of studying the psychological aspects of performance. I've had the opportunity to play regularly with a golfer who eventually won multiple PGA tournaments. And, although I'm far removed from that expertise, I've played in more best-ball invitational tournaments than I can remember. None of this is meant to impress you because it really doesn't matter how I can play but more on how I can interact with you and share very useful information that I guarantee will improve your putting IF (and this I hope will turn to WHEN) you deliberately take some of the many necessary steps I outline. You'll be exposed to many persuasions, strategies, and drills. Every golfer is different, and there are many options that you can choose to achieve OUR mutual intended goal TO PUTT BETTER.

What this book does NOT deal with:

It does NOT deal with putting mechanics—grip, stance, head position, stroke plane, etc. These items are dealt with in numerous other books on golf generally and putting specifically. If you are interested in the argument of which putting stroke is better, then read Stan Utley's description and support of *arc putting* and compare it to Dave Pelz' *straight back, straight through approach*. This is useful information, and clearly one cannot putt successfully without a solid stroke, but mechanics is, as they say today, "beyond my pay grade."

It does NOT deal with equipment choice, although I clearly have my favorite. But, then again, like you I've had <u>many favorites</u> through the years, and we've rotated them in and out of play quite regularly, haven't we? After all, a period of "time out" is an appropriate cure for bad behavior. On the contrary, good putters seem like they could even putt with a tree limb. What's important is that you love the putter you're using.

It does NOT deal with stories of professional golfers' successes following psychological intervention or golf putting gurus' lessons.

It is NOT intended to be a know-it-all treatise on the psychological aspects of putting nor is it intended to be the last word.

And, last, the content is NOT all mine, not by a long shot. Nobody can lay claim to having the last word on all the issues that impact putting success, although some come closer than others. For example, nobody even approaches the legacy of Dave Pelz with the vast amount of research he and his colleagues have conducted on various aspects of putting. You might be interested in looking at Marius Filmalter's

Automatic Putting DVD Set based on his over 20 years of putting research.

Who and what is this book written FOR:

It is FOR the everyman golfer—male or female, young or old, serious or recreational, amateur or professional—everyone who would like to putt better. Young beginning golfers can begin to lay down a solid base for a lifetime of putting success. Recreational golfers can pick up some tips to clip a couple of strokes off their game and add to their fun. The game can be fun, can't it? Even the best golfers in the world struggle with their putting. I bet there's not a single golfer on the PGA, LPGA, and European tours that is really happy with his or her putting statistics. They all feel they could and should do better, and I would certainly echo their sentiments.

It is FOR the correction of common putting issues all golfers must deal with. For example, how do we golfers deal with our missed putts that nobody should miss?

It is FOR the establishment of a framework underlying putting success, not just a bunch of isolated "sound bites." This framework will provide a useful filter as you judge the validity of what you read in golf magazines and what you hear from golf instructors, golf commentators, and especially your golfing partners.

It is FOR the translation of the best information derived from putting experts, psychology, neuropsychology, learning theory, and other areas into applied/usable form. You might wonder if indeed there is a science of putting, because after all "putting isn't brain science." Or, is it? I think you'll change your mind on this point once you get into the book and began to decide where you might need to do some mental adjustments.

It is FOR every golfer to find their pet putting problem(s) and consider the nature of the solution(s) offered. For example, why does a missed putt linger throughout the round? This might sound a little presumptuous on my part but I believe in my many years of playing golf I have suffered at times through pretty much most of the putting ills all golfers face. And if the whole truth were to be known, I still struggle with certain aspects. I've come to the conclusion that all golfers are merely works-in-progress. Don't you agree?

It is FOR convincing golfers to consider, explore, develop, and employ the many approaches, thinking, understanding, strategies, and drills contained herein.

I am indebted to those who have given me insight into and beyond my own personal golfing experiences, especially David Cook, Patrick Cohn, Joe Parent, Dave Pelz, Bob Rotella, Stan Utley, and Robert Winters. As they say, "imitation is the sincerest form of flattery," and I have shared some of these authors' thoughts, sometimes blatantly, with you the readers of this book. In some instances, their thoughts were better than mine, and I highly recommend their books to you. At other times, I found I had to take exception with another's particular assertion, but I hope I did it with respect because others' ideas have fostered my own learning. Particularly, I want to thank Karl Pribram, whose *Languages of the Brain* has captured my attention for the past 30 years. It is his work primarily that has given me an opportunity to peer into how the brain functions to create the many plans of action that play themselves out on the putting green (and everywhere else I might add).

Allow me to direct a plea to all of you who are parents and grandparents of aspiring golfers. I STRONGLY URGE you to read one or both of the following books: Geoff Colvin's *Talent is Overrated* and Daniel Coyle's *The Talent Code*. Please don't misunderstand my intention here. All I want you to do is grasp the framework underlying the development of expertise and impart this in the doses you see fit. A brief outline of deliberate practice is outlined in this book but reading from the original sources will offer you a complete picture of how to set up the kind of practice that will get results, especially if you're trying to help a novice golfer. There's so little we know about practice as evident by how we go about it. Much of what we do is copied from others without much thought of purpose and outcome. And speaking about results, should it be much of a surprise when our usual putting practice doesn't transfer to on-course putting?

The reader is encouraged to complete The Top 10 Reasons Why Golfers Sabotage Their Putting Success inventory to calculate your personal sabotage index. The first three chapters of the book deal with the difficulties inherent in the putting process and set the stage for understanding and dealing with the issues raised. The fourth chapter explains how intentional putting plans are created and why putting really is brain science. The fifth chapter offers strategies and drills to solve the mystery of reading greens. Most, if not all, of the problems golfers face are explained and remedies are offered in chapter six. The seventh chapter deals with the development of putting competence and confidence, with a focus on the four major building blocks: concentration, commitment, control, and consistency, which are dealt with individually in chapters eight through eleven. The book concludes with a brief summary, the Ten Commandments of Putting, and an epilog.

ONE. PUTTING IS NOT FAIR

Golf is the cruelest of sports. Like life, it's unfair. It's a harlot. A trollop. It leads you on. It never lives up to its promises. It's a boulevard of broken dreams. It plays with men. And runs off with the butcher. Jim Murray, prominent sports writer

Perhaps the harshest reality for all of us to accept is that NOTHING about golf is fair. The real dilemma is to accept the fact that the game we love (or "hate") to play is rooted in the unfairness doctrine and that it will always be thus. To the degree that any us fight this truth, we cast our lot with the insane and will tend to behave accordingly.

If golf was intended to be fair:

* You wouldn't have to hit your lifetime best tee ball out of somebody else's ditch-size divot in the middle of the fairway.

* The rules of golf wouldn't insist that you have to identify your totally buried and invisible ball in a bunker, and then return it to its sandy grave before attempting to extricate it.

* Golf architects would have more consideration for you by not placing trees in your intended line to the greens or by not building greens on dinosaur burial grounds.

* You wouldn't have a worse lie missing a narrow fairway by a mere 2 feet than your opponent who drives his ball two fairways left and has a wide open shot to the green from an impeccable lie.

Need I continue? You see what I mean—golf isn't fair and putting is the least fair of all as the following points will substantiate.

1. Not all well-read and well-struck putts go in, and some poorly read and poorly struck putts miraculously do fall in. I'm sure you've had more than one occasion when it seemed impossible for your putt to miss but it encircled the hole, danced the 360, looked back at you, and haughtily exclaimed: "No putt's a sure thing." And all your partners cried in unison, "You were robbed—that wasn't fair." Conversely, you've struck putts that NEVER seemed to be on line but they got to the edge of the hole and toppled over into the hole. And your golfing partners, realizing the unfairness to themselves, cried in unison, "You lucky stiff (or some expletive)—you didn't deserve that putt."

2. Some putts hit imperfections in the greens, such as spike marks, unrepaired or poorly repaired ball marks, faulty cut lines, etc., you didn't or couldn't see. And, even if you could have seen them, the rules of golf would have prohibited you from tamping some of them down. Now, how fair is that? A large twisting and mountainous spike mark left by an previous golfer places your routine 3-footer in jeopardy. Also, it just doesn't seem right that retirees get the luxury of early morning smooth greens while the poor working stiffs get the late afternoon and early evening bumpy green surfaces, especially when the latter are subsidizing the former's green fees through social security payments. That seems doubly unfair to me. (However, as an "experienced" golfer myself, I have to accept such an inequity, but understand I do so with regrets!).

3. The cups on the greens are ALWAYS raised higher than the surrounding surfaces, and many putts fail to navigate that last partial rotation and hang on the lip or curl away at the last second. Sometimes this is the fault of the maintenance crew who raise the edges of the cup when cutting the hole. But, much more commonly, putts are left short because of what Dave Pelz calls the "lumpy donut" effect. No, this isn't a castigation on golfers' physiques but a real, true-to-life effect. As golfers step in to lift their made putts out of the holes, they create a circular and lumpy indentation about 6 inches from the hole. This leaves the cup slightly (depending on the softness of the greens and the tonnage of the previous golfers) higher than the surrounding putting surface. The result is that all putts need to climb out of the indentation to get to the hole. Who knew? Thanks Dave!

4. Not all putts break the same from similar locations on the green. Who amongst us can't recall getting what we thought was a great read from a partner's putt only to have our subsequent putt fail to break or break more than was expected? It seemed like a sure thing, or as close to a sure thing as the game offers. You shake your head, bemoan your outcast state in your own personal ways, and chalk it up to how unfair putting is. Even "guarantees" aren't guaranteed!

5. It doesn't seem fair when you're playing against someone who "bunts" the ball down the fairway, seldom gets to the green in regulation, chips up, and then sinks the putt for a par, whereas you in all your magnificence crush your drive, fly a majestic iron into the green, and then have to 2-putt from 25 feet for a tie on the hole. Your mind just won't allow you to see the equivalence of these diverse scenarios and, what's more unfair, unless you somehow find a way to resolve this dilemma, you're doomed to the hell of mental unfairness. Your mental block notwithstanding, you are forced to accept the short hitter's/great putter's well-worn, supercilious smiling cliche: "There are no pictures on the scorecard, only numbers." Or, "It doesn't matter how you arrive, only the final score counts." GRRR! Good putters drive good ball strikers crazy, don't they? Even the great Bobby Jones griped about this inequity: *When a man misses a drive, and misses his second shot, and wins the hole with a birdie—it gets my goat.* Right on, Bobby!

6. What's one of the worst things that can happen to you? You hit the longest drive, see everybody hit their second shot on the green, and now it's your turn. And even to compound the pressure you place on your putter and your mind, what happens if everybody ends up closer to the hole than you? Now you run the "what, if . . ." dialog. "What, if after such a great drive, I don't par the hole?" Is it fair to place this much pressure on your putting, and why should putting count so much? If you ever hear yourself emit such self-talking, then you're eligible to be a bona fide member of the Ben Hogan fan club whose namesake often argued: *Hitting a golf ball and putting have nothing in common. They're two different games. You work all your life to perfect a repeating swing that will get you to the greens, and then you have to try something that is totally unrelated. There shouldn't be any cups, just flagsticks. And the man who hits the most fairways and greens and*

got closest to the pins would be the tournament winner. Nobody in the golfing hierarchy would listen!

7. Of all the real estate on the greens, why does the superintendent choose to set the pins so close to the edges of greens, just beside gaping bunkers? If there's only one mound on the green, is it just by chance the pin gets set either on top of the mound or just on the back side of the mound? What's this all about? Does superintendent school teach that pins should be set on side hill slopes? If so, the course must be titled Sadism 101! These "questionable" decisions create a sense of desperation in golfers who are trying their best to be confident in the face of already difficult odds. Even under the best putting conditions, <u>most putts are missed</u>. This tips golfers over the edge and fosters a whining and begging attitude (unfortunately not accommodated

Reprinted by permission of Finkstrom Licensing International.

by our unanimously hard-hearted playing partners). You know what a "gimme" is, don't you? It's an agreement between golfers, neither of whom putt very well.

8. And, what help do we get from the various golf experts and golf professionals? Steve Rushin (*Golf Digest*, October 2010) shares with us his frustration *that the best the pros can do is to tell us how to miss. Miss it on the pro side, they say, meaning miss it above the hole.* Like most golfers, we miss it short, we blast it long, we miss it high, and we leave it low. *Worst of all*, Rushin commiserates, *I'm famous for missing it precisely where the hole <u>used</u> to be. My ball comes to rest within that circular seam where the previous hole was just plugged, and I stare at my putterface in disbelief. That face always stares back, unblinking, unmoved.* Have you been there? Do you ever just slap your putterface or feel the urge to bend the shaft over your knee? Or more?

In the *Golf Digest* issue referenced above, the witty and humorous (and sometimes irreverent) golf writer, Dan Jenkins, offers us a nice summation to explain our putting difficulties:

> *The golf ball has no sense at all, which is why it has to be given stern lectures constantly, especially during the act of putting . . . . The golf ball thinks it has assumed a more important role after it reaches the green that is because, as Ben Hogan taught us, putting has nothing to with playing golf. That's why the golf ball tends to fight back on the greens after being whacked around on the fairway, in the trees, and bunkers, and rock piles, and whatever have you. Putting is where the golf ball considers it will get even.*

Several of the many tasks I've set out for myself in this book is to challenge the "apparent" wisdom and rationale of just how unfair putting is and to offer persuasive arguments and possible solutions to the task of putting so that you might begin to approach the attitude of one of the all-time acknowledged great putters, Dave Stockton, who exclaimed: *I never met a putt I couldn't make.* Of course, he missed thousands of putts, but his attitude and approach was one of planning and intending to make each putt no matter the eventual outcome. That's the positive approach to putting and the only approach that will maximize your chances for improvement. If this path appeals to you, and you feel that you can become a better putter, then there's many opportunities in the book to allow you to move in the direction of being more proficient on the greens. Come along! The trip will be well worth your time.

TWO. THE HARSH REALITIES OF PUTTING

Golf is an ineffectual attempt to put an elusive ball into an obscure hole with implements ill-adapted for the purpose. Woodrow Wilson

All golfers recognize the oft-heard assertion: "Drive for show and putt for dough." Is this the truth? Is putting the most important aspect of golf? Don't we admire the 300+ yard tee shots that pro golfers hit fairly routinely? What about those shots into greens that dance around and settle inches from the hole? Don't those "impossible" (if you listen to the expert commentators) trouble shots bring you up off the couch? Phil and Tiger have given us enough of these to last us a couple of lifetimes, and I'm sure there are more to come in the future.

Dave Pelz, the short game guru and compiler of multitudes of putting data based on carefully planned and controlled research, informs us that 43% (+/-2%) of ALL golfers' scores is derived from putting. This applies to the best golfers in the world right down to the least of us. That's two out of every five strokes. Do your own calculation. What do you regularly shoot? Calculate the number of putts normally made. That's a fairly large number, isn't it? In 18 holes you will successfully make 18 putts, unless you hole out from the fairway or fringe (and don't we wish we could do this more often?) and miss the remainder. If you shoot 90, applying the 43% equation above, on average you will take 37 putts (i.e., make 18 + miss 19 = 37 putts). Allow me to shed some light on the dark side of putting.

1. Putting seems to be the easiest part of golf but, in reality, it's the hardest. Sure the target is small (4.25 inches in diameter) but there's plenty of room for error (the golf ball is only 1.68 inches in diameter). The hole has room for 2.5 golf balls entering simultaneously. The grass on the putting green is cut short and rolled fairly smooth, not like the fairways and roughs we play from. There are no trees, bunkers, or other architectural ploys (other than mounds) in our putting lines. The

distance from ball to hole is quite short compared to most other shots. Golfers get to see the breaks of putts and forces needed to traverse particular distances from their golfing partners. Unlike other shots, in putting there's a clear target, even accentuated by a partner holding the flagstick, if so desired. I believe if you asked someone who had zero knowledge about the game of golf (i.e., never heard of golf, never saw golf being played, etc.) to predict which was more difficult, hitting a small ball with strangely configured implements through a tunnel of trees to a mown target 400 yards away versus hitting a small ball into an oversized hole from a distance of 12 feet, I think you'd find that putting would be judged the easier. Such was the case when the great pool player, Joe Davis, saw his first game of golf. The putting puzzled him. *Why,* he asked his experienced golfing friend, *don't they knock the ball into the hole the first time?* This just exemplifies one of the many confusing paradoxes of golf.

2. The only way to record good scores (the ones you're willing to talk about) is by good putting. You've heard it said many times: "Putting is the great equalizer. It's the great eraser; all is forgiven if the putt drops." It makes all your other shots easier when you excel on the greens—previous shots don't need to be perfect. No score on the hole is finalized until the putt drops. The sliced drive into the trees is painful, the punch out woefully short of the green is disappointing, the wedge a pathetic 30 feet from the pin particularly unnerving, but the exhilarating holed par putt is really all that matters. All is forgiven. Conversely, poor putting can nullify a great drive, long and in the middle of the fairway, and a crisp 4-iron into the heart of the green 10 feet from the pin. The unforgivable 3-putt undermines the success of the previous shots. I guess that's why good putters smile a lot and poor putters are perpetual whiners. I hope you grasp the not-so-subtle message—putting is singly the most important stroke in golf—and the more often you can keep it in the singular (i.e., 1-putt) on each hole rather than in the plural, the better will be your score and ultimately your attitude.

3. Not all good putts go in. You know this already and you'll acknowledge the following obvious reasons: the ball gets deflected by some imperfection on the green; the break flattened just as the ball neared the hole; or the ball looked in but "decided" to remain aloft.

Because we golfers are so creative in explaining our misses, I'm sure you could add to my abbreviated list. Or do you believe that unless the putt goes in it's not a good putt? If so, you're destined to be at least disappointed and at worse outraged: "How could this happen to me? That putt was perfect."

4. Research shows that even tour players make only 50% of their 6-footers. NO, you can't believe this, can you? You watch professional golf on TV and you see putts of all lengths just filling the hole, way more than 50%. But, what you don't see are all the putts by all the golfers from Thursdays to Sundays. I can assure you the percentage is correct. What does this mean for you? You should make all your 6-footers and shorter on greens less well manicured than those on which the professional golfers play? Be serious! Get real! Understand the realities of putting!

5. All golfers sabotage their chances for putting success by poor mechanics, faulty green reading, poor pre-putt routines and rituals, and crazy thinking. You know what I mean by crazy thinking because you hear your inner thoughts "verbalized" all the time: "Don't 3-putt"; "Don't leave it short"; "At least get it to the hole." Nod your head if you're with me, but not so anybody else will notice! These are things that will be addressed later to provide some insights and alterations that you can make to achieve greater putting success.

6. We would all be better putters if we hit our iron shots closer to the hole. As obvious and intuitive as this statement is, proximity to the hole is the "secret" to good putting. And, furthermore, if we could routinely get our first putt inside 6 feet, we'd undoubtedly reduce our putting stats. But, that's not likely to happen very often is it, and that might even be a bigger challenge than making a first long putt. So, a nice thought, but put another check mark beside the inevitability of reality.

7. Have you noticed that birdie putts are more difficult to make than par putts, and also that bogey putts are easier to make than par putts? Do you think this just a function of distance from the hole? How do you find the 4-foot birdie putts? Nearly guaranteed? And what do

notice about the par putts you run way past the hole? The come-back putts for bogey don't seem

Reprinted by permission of Finkstrom Licensing International.

that difficult to make, do they? The point I'm making here is that the more important the putt, the more difficult it will be to make because it means so much. This is just a given unless you believe in and implement some of the strategies you'll find later in this book. The problem is not mechanical, rather it is psychological. Putting is a mind game, way more than a physical challenge.

8. So far I think you'll agree that putting is very important to your overall golf score, but here's the "rest of the story." Putting not only accounts for a little over 40% of your golf score but likely more than 80% of the frustration and aggravation you feel from your golfing

Reprinted by permission of Finkstrom Licensing International.

experience. This reminds me of Peter Dobereiner's assertion: *Half of golf is fun; the other half is putting.* What part of the game do you enjoy practicing? Don't tell me. Hitting the driver? Is there a message here? You would rather spend your practice time working the kinks out of a club you will likely hit no more than 14 times a round but give little more than lip service to a club that literally will have the greatest impact on your score every day you play? (Of course, excluding the days you blow it out bounds with some regularity). Let me continue to add to the list of harsh realities that have negative psychological ramifications.

9. There appears to be a great mismatch between golfers' mindsets and the task demands of putting. Putting is often claimed to be 90% psychological but we golfers tend to be mental lightweights. One of my golfing buddies, Biff, taught me a new term to apply to ourselves when we make a boneheaded error, that being MO-RON. Yes, we golfers certainly do some stupid things in our futile attempts to achieve

putting success. My hope is that you'll find a few things in this book that will improve your putting IQ and move you up the achievement ladder. I believe there will be something for everybody!

10. Maybe you and I are wiser than it would appear when we spend most of our practice time on the driving range and so little time on the practice putting green. The putting practice we do doesn't seem to make us better putters, nor does reading random putting tips in golf magazines, nor does purchasing "better" putters with strange looking and mysterious sounding face inserts and scientifically engineered MOI's (moment of inertia, to those of you who normally aren't seduced by such terminology). Just the other day I heard that golf handicaps hadn't changed in 30 years. Can that be? We play on better manicured greens, we have more "how-to-putt" literature and short game schools, and we have better engineered putters. Also, we hit the ball farther, hit shorter clubs into greens, and have better maintained bunkers. What would make the single most decrease in our handicaps? If you answered, PUTT BETTER, then you've aced the question. The reality is that we either don't know the essentials of good putting or we don't apply them (if the latter, then we really are MO-RONS). My intent is to offer you the best suggestions that I believe are available in the hope that you will be in the forefront of changing the 30-year old statistic. Essentially I'll be trying to round off the rough edges of putting reality and bring some smoothness to your putting stroke.

11. You will likely make as many or more putts in a round of golf than you miss. Do the math. Two putts a hole equals 36 putts. More than likely you'll have less. So, by deduction, you make more putts than you miss. But the reality is irrelevant because of selective or mismanaged memory. Listen to a typical discussion in the 19th hole following a round of golf and see if this dialog is at all familiar? "You wouldn't believe how many of my putts just burned the edges today"; "If I could putt, I could play this game"; "I bet I had four 3-putt greens today"; "I missed a birdie putt on the 3rd hole that had to be less than 3 feet"; "The putts just weren't breaking today." I know these are all familiar to you and I'll bet you could double, triple, or quadruple this list. In fact, if you come across some really unique "reasons" for so-called bad putting, please send them to me. But, to return to my main point, you see that golfers tend to focus on the putts they <u>miss</u>

rather than on the putts they <u>make</u>, which of course just adds to the harsh reality of putting and keeps the downward spiral spinning. Surely you understand the psychological cost for accentuating your lack of skill and success. Even your occasional good putting days don't usually carry that much weight on your putting psyche. Putting confidence is a fleeting thing!

12. Much will be said of the role that confidence plays in putting success later in the book, but let me make one major and blatantly obvious point now. Confidence is based to a large extent on making putts, but the reality is most first putts and a lot of important putts are missed. Without some intervention or proper interpretation on your part, the outcome of a missed putt will be a loss of confidence. That's why I join others like pro golfer David Frost in recommending that you not miss any more pre-round practice putts than necessary, avoiding those long putts that most everyone misses. Recall my earlier point about the success rate of putts as short as 6 feet. Putt the 3-5 footers to build your putting confidence rather than eroding your confidence with inevitable misses. Remember this point but you'll hear much more about it later: Every made or missed putt is deposited in your putting bank account, really in your brain's association cortex, from which memory for future putts is derived. I hope this sounds as scary to you as it does to me! Memory bank overdrafts are not possible; but you do get to spend what you accrue.

13. In light of the above, a further point needs to be added. Missed short putts kill confidence the most and have an infectious effect not only on future putts but also on the rest of your game. How long would it take <u>you</u> to get over an obvious birdie "gimme" putt you missed on the first green that eventually turned into a 3-putt? I'm reminded of a recent incident I had on the course. It was one of my partner's turn to tee off and I asked him what was holding him up as he was "fiddling around" on the tee. He replied, "I'm still putting on the last hole," and then he promptly hit his tee shot out-of-bounds. I'll bet we've all been there! Putting is the last thing golfers do before they move on to the next hole. If the memory residue of a recent poor putting performance haunts your consciousness as you prepare to strike your next tee shot, look out! Trouble is waiting for you to make it happen. It doesn't just occur, you're the maestro of this orchestration and the outcome

will not be met by applause (at least not by you). And, there's no consolation that a bad shot always pleases someone, is there?

14. One of the realities of golf generally and putting specifically is the amount of time in a round of golf spent in NOT striking the golf ball. Somebody with too much time on their hands, I suspect, has claimed that we spend much less than 3 minutes actually hitting our shots. However, that time frame might increase depending on how many strokes you take. Unlike some other free-flowing sports like basketball, soccer, tennis, etc., the time between shots becomes the golfer's enemy. Golf is a game of stops and starts, mostly stops. Because you're not running around (your golfing partners would frown on this), you stand around with your ever-generating thoughts (e.g., "Does my putt break right or left: I can't read it"), and the waiting can be extremely dangerous. Sometimes by the time it's finally your turn to putt, it's a wonder you can even take the putter away from the ball. You've rehearsed so many fundamentals, given yourself multiple admonishments, and checked and double-checked your read that the putt takes on a life of its own. Intelligent golfers have ways of filling this down time with useful preparatory routines that allow them the greatest chance of making their putt.

15. And lastly, in the scheme of things, putting seems to count too much. A 1/4-inch leaning tap-in putt counts the same as a 275-yard drive. Really? The Scots who invented or at least popularized the game must have been numerically deficient. But, this is the game we love

Reprinted by permission of Finkstrom Licensing International.

. . . or love to hate. Putting is rather like being a hockey, soccer, or lacrosse goaltender—a miss by the goalie counts one and immediately goes on the scoreboard with no chance of it being erased. No do-overs like in tennis. Errors made prior to arriving at the green (e.g., driving into the woods, chunking your iron shot, chili-dipping your wedge, etc.) can all be forgiven by a great putt. But a failed putt cannot be overcome—the "ball stops here."

Looking over the above leads me to ask a number of questions. Why would we commit so much of our time and effort to such a pastime with such harsh realities and the capacity for so much aggravation? And why, when it's so obvious that putting is the keystone to good scoring, don't we rationally proportion our practice time to the relative importance of each part of the game? Is it because our putting practice doesn't seem to matter—we never get better? Is our lack of putting success mechanical or is putting really a psychological exercise? Perhaps golfers are really masochists who derive enjoyment out of the possibility of the elusive highlights interspersed so rarely among the preponderance of mediocre or horrible shots. Golf is no place for the perfectionist.* Even Ben Hogan who is still revered as the preeminent shotmaker claimed that he only hit one or two great shots in an entire round of golf. Well, I believe the answer why we play golf lies in the infectious nature of the game and in the pursuit of our own "perfection," even though in our rational moments we really know we're up against it. But it's those few great shots or the odd great sequence of holes that keep us coming back for more. If only we could maximize our greatness and minimize our frailties, then we would enjoy the game even more. Although the better we get, the higher will be our expectations and the cycle will just continue. You can never beat the game of golf, the best you can do is co-exist with it and accept the consequences of your choice. On a more positive note, however, I'm optimistic that I can get you thinking a little better and leave you with some strategies and drills for lowered scoring and an improved attitude toward the game.

---

* Unless, of course, you are driven to be great, what psychologist Ellen Winner calls the *rage to master*. Only a few people possess this quality, and if you've got to ask, you don't have it. Ben Hogan was a perfectionist, and I suspect Tiger Woods and Vijay Singh also belong to this elite class.

THREE. FACTORS THAT IMPACT PUTTING SUCCESS

In golf, driving is a game of free swing muscle control, while putting is something like performing eye surgery and using a bread knife for a scalpel. Tommy Bolt

It rather goes without saying that no golfer is truly happy with his or her putting statistics. All of us would like to putt better, and most of us believe that we can putt better. We look at the statistics from even the best players in the world (90% success from 3 feet, 50% from 6 feet, 30% from 9 feet, 20% from 12 feet, 10% from 20 feet, and 5% from 30 feet) and realize that our statistics aren't nearly this good. Putting doesn't look this difficult but the statistics don't lie. What are the essentials of putting success? What holds us back? Why can't the best players in the world, for whom golf is their livelihood, putt better? And yet, upon reflection, on those rare days when we string two or three or even four birdies together, we are perfect and nobody in the world could have done better. Why can't we do this more often? The success equation is complex, multidimensional, and very daunting but hopefully you're prepared to wade through the following laundry list.

Condition of Greens

As I found on moving from the northeast to the southeast and then to the southwest, **grain** plays a significant role on the speed and break of the putted ball. Until you've putted on bermuda greens when you're always been used to bent greens, you can't appreciate the impact of putting into the grain and down grain. Putts fly down grain and roll sluggishly up grain. Professional golfers even have trouble adjusting when the tour swings from California to Florida because of the green changes. The **slope** of greens adds to the difficulty as I'm sure you can attest when you play a course with "elephant burial grounds" used as greens. Much of your putting experience becomes unraveled in situations like this. Another factor that must be considered is the **surface** of the green. Is it smooth or rough? Is it even or uneven? Are there a lot of poorly repaired ballmarks or have your predecessors been conscientious in their green maintenance? Is the surface damp or dry? Is the green hard as pavement or so soft it leaves footprints? In repairing your ballmark, does your repair tool easily fix the mark or is the surface more like concrete? Golfers have to account for numerous conditions in preparing their putting strategy. Failure to incorporate key cues and discard irrelevant cues dooms <u>every</u> putt.

Green Reading

With all the variables listed above it's understandable that putts will be misread. But the reality is that misread putts will never be successful. Greens are misread for a variety or reasons: golfers don't pick out the task-relevant cues, golfers see but don't act on the cues correctly, golfers casually glance at a general putting target and aimline without considering a specific plan of action, or golfers don't even know the essence of reading greens. No matter how good your putting stroke, without a conscious effort to select the correct cues and discard the irrelevant cues, you will never be better than a poor putter.

Distance Control

Accuracy of reading greens, however, is of little use if golfers can't match ball direction, ball speed, and distance. On a breaking putt, for example, there are dozens of correct targets and aimlines depending on the speed of the putt. In fact, the break of the putt cannot be accurately read without simultaneously considering how hard you intend to stroke the putt. You wouldn't likely be comfortable choosing Tiger Woods' targets and aimlines for downhill breaking putts because undoubtedly you're not a consistently bold putter as he is. You might play more break and allow the putt to just trickle over the top edge, a la Jack Nicklaus. Distance control has to be learned through experience, although most golfers don't work on specific drills to ingrain the feel needed to control distance. Ask yourself if you could accurately putt a ball 10 feet on a flat green, adjust to a 10-foot downhill putt, and then adjust to a 10-foot uphill putt, all on the same green? What about other distances? That's the key to controlling distance, building in the feeling of the force (i.e., touch or feel) needed for each putt.

Accuracy of Irons

Excuse me for being obvious again, but the closer the ball is to the hole, the greater the likelihood of a 1-putt. Go back and reread the opening paragraph to see how putting percentages decline with distance from the hole. On the other hand, whether you hit your iron shot much outside 15 or 20 feet doesn't matter that much. You're probably looking at a 2-putt, maybe even more. Earlier I indicated that putting comprises a little over 40% of all golfers' scores to convince you of the proportional significance of putting. Now consider the importance of pitching and chipping the ball close to the hole to your overall putting stats and overall score. If you could only practice two aspects of the game, what would they be? Of course, PUTTING first and PITCHING/CHIPPING second. But, what do we golfers complain about at our home course or at the away courses we play? "There's no room on the range to hit drivers." So what! Practice the scoring clubs!

Pre-putt Routine and Ritual

A plan of action needs some systematization for time, thoroughness, and sequence. There's little if any chance of producing a confident feeling as you stand over the putt unless you've "dotted the i's and crossed the t's." That's a cliche but one that truly applies to putting. You need to standardize your pre-putt preparation, do all the work before you prepare to stroke the putt, and then turn the outcome over to trust. Ask yourself this question as it applies to the work you do or to other endeavors you pursue: When do you really trust that you're going to be able to achieve the outcome you'd like? I'll wager that it's when you've done all the "homework," both quantitatively and qualitatively, that's possible and you have a feeling of anticipation rather than worry. Am I close? You see, putting is like life, only harder!

Putting Competence/Confidence

Competence is the factually-based "knowledge" of how well you typically putt, whereas confidence is the positive feeling you have as you stand over a putt. Competence is based on how good a putter you are, based mainly on your past performance. Confidence is a little more of a day-to-day (or even a hole-to-hole, or a putt-to-putt) commodity depending on your ability to control a situation's particular demands and commit to a solid plan of action without second guessing yourself. It's like double jeopardy if you're generally not a very competent putter and you are susceptible to the daily ebbs and flows of putting outcomes (e.g., putts lip out, putts don't break as expected, short putts are missed, putts get thrown off line by green imperfections, playing partners reminding you of recent missed putts, etc.). You know without me telling you that confidence at the moment of truth is the key to performance, and that there can be no real confidence without underlying competence to perform the task. And, yet, putting competence will only be realized if your approach takes on a confident air. How would you ever know how good a putter you could become if you never had confidence in your putting? Later on you'll read how Vijah Singh turned his putting statistics around. Our assessment of how well we putt is constrained by our degree of putting confidence.

Visualization

As you prepare to putt, do you see a specific spot on the green that your intended putt must target if you're to have any chance of success? And, do you "see" the track or path the ball needs to travel to be successful? I mean actually visualize the track as if it was painted on the green like the imaginary lines you see on football telecasts to indicate the distance required for first downs or the ones you see on golf telecasts. "Seeing is believing," as the adage asserts, and there's real truth behind the claim. For golfers, Jack Nicklaus popularized the concept of visualization, although I'm positive that great golfers of all eras created "pictures" of their shots long before Jack rose to prominence. In *Golf My Way*, Nicklaus described his pre-shot preparation this way: *I never hit a shot, even in practice, without having a very sharp, in-focus picture of it in my head* [Wow! Are you reading this? Never . . . not even in practice?]. *It's like a color movie. First, I 'see' the ball where I want it to finish* [outcome] . . . . *Then the scene quickly changes and I 'see'* [visualize] *the ball going there; its path, trajectory and shape, even its behavior on landing.* These "home movies" were the key to Jack's concentration and pre-shot preparation. When you watch televised golf tournaments, what do you suppose professional golfers are doing when they stand behind the ball staring intently to seek out their intended aimlines? Correct. They're visualizing the track the ball will travel, even painting imaginary lines from the ball to the hole. If only they could see the computer-generated lines televised golf audiences are privy to see. Failure for you and I to harness our power of visualization means that we're missing a key element in our pre-putt preparation, and we will pay for our misdeeds in reduced putting proficiency. It's so much easier to make a confident putting stroke when you can "see" the ball travel on your intended path and finally drop into the cup.

Self-talking

Your brain is turned on at birth and turned off at death, and your mind is constantly jabbering in the background. It will always be thus! But, when the content of your inner dialog turns negative, the caution flag needs to go up immediately followed by the STOP sign. Maybe you've never considered the impact self-talk has on your performance but you've undoubtedly reaped its impact. Picture yourself driving to a new destination, following directions given to you by a golfing friend. What's going on it your head as you drive? "Go to the 3rd light and turn right on Elm St. Look for the Wendy's on the right a few blocks up and make a left on Maple. Go past two gas stations and start looking for the entrance to the Northview Mall. The PGA Superstore is way at the back to your left." You rehearse this dialog, piece by piece, as you reach and pass each checkpoint. Why do you do such a thing? Simply because it works! Often, however, without specific directions and knowledge of how to construct our own dialog about our putting, for example, our self-talk turns negative with not surprisingly negative outcomes. Consider some typical examples of negative self-talk about your putting mechanics, putting outcome, and your putting competence: "Keep your grip loose and don't jab at the ball."; "I really need to make this one or I lose the hole."; "There's no chance of making this putt the way I've putting today; Let's just get it close and not embarrass myself." Self-talking will always occur, it's your choice to control the direction—positive or negative. What's the alternative? Turn your putting performance over to an irrational, spontaneous, and disordered thought process? That's insanity!

Emotional Control

Think of all the possible emotions you could have as you prepare to stroke your putt—anticipation, arousal, anxiety, fear, loathing, and likely a horde of other feelings. The more emotional or excited (positively or negatively) you are, the more likely you are to lose some control of your entire putting plan of action. You'll tend to speed up and this will play havoc with your rhythm and tempo. Even your normal vigilant green reading process and certainly your feel for distance will be hampered. Accentuating the importance of the outcome rather than trusting your plan to achieve the goal puts the "cart before the horse," so to speak. Denigrating your competence is sheer madness. Why even bother putting? Ask your partners to give you a score and start for home. You're like the person who says "Stick a fork in me, I'm done."

Recent Putting Outcomes

It's seems to be so natural to correct a current plan of action based on a recent negative outcome, doesn't it? Why would anyone in their right mind continue doing something that doesn't work? That's insanity, or so it seems. But let's consider two major points. First, what contributed to a recently missed putt? And second, what are the key ingredients for achieving a successful outcome? Any previous putt could have been missed for any number of reasons, many of them unrelated to the current putting plan, namely distance from the hole, contour of the green, condition of the green, poor read, mechanical glitch in the stroke, attitude, or some outside factor. To give yourself the best chance of making the current putt my suggestion is not even to plug the memory of a recently missed putt into the current equation. I know, easier said than done! Go through your standard pre-putt routine, recall a putt like this made before, and putt with a sense that you'll make a good stroke. Think about this for a moment and ask yourself this question: "What other alternative do I have?" None! Do we really CONTROL the outcome, or is the outcome based partially on what we do and partially on what gravity does? What control do we have once the putted ball leaves the putter? NONE. It makes little sense to attempt to putt confidently based on all the negative ramifications of a previously missed putt. Does this compute or resonate with you? I hope so. Would you rather putt out of a sense of failure or a sense of success?

Outside Factors

Sometimes as you're about to putt, you're caught unaware by a sudden noise in the background. A lawn mower starts up, a partner coughs or sneezes, a nearby gas-powered golf cart backfires, or somebody from the group in front of you celebrates loudly over a made putt. The startle response kicks in and your normally smooth flowing putting stroke disintegrates. The noise could be intentional as the old ploy of jingling coins in the pocket is played out by one of your "friends." This does not startle you as much as it diverts your attention from your routine and mindset. Sometimes your golfing partners are wont to remind you of your putting weaknesses: "We're safe,

Reprinted by permission of Finkstrom Licensing International.

he can't make short putts." This plays into the psyche of a golfer who has an acknowledged penchant for missing short putts, and you might even hear him make a derogatory remark about himself or his putting if he misses the short putt. Most likely he's either planning his response as he makes his stroke or he's already preplanned his "obituary". The point of all of this is that stuff happens. Control it, reframe it, dismiss it if possible, and return to your plan. If it's not controllable, then it's a bad break and, I guess, another aspect of "rub of the green" that all golfers must live with.

Learning vs. Performance Issues

It's important to understand the reason(s) for your lack of putting success and not attribute it to false factors. Perhaps the reason you had so many 3-putts yesterday was that you never got your first putt close enough to the hole to make the next one. Was it your lack of distance control or your inability to make 3- to 5-foot putts? Are these learning problems or performance problems? You need to figure this out after the round is over and act accordingly. Take the distance control problem: If you never practice putts of different lengths from flat, uphill, downhill, and sidehill lies, then it's a **learning** problem and you need to spend some quality time on the practice putting green with a specific agenda in mind. If you tighten up your grip over long putts because they cause you to fear the outcome, then it's a **performance** problem. Now consider the 3- to 5-foot putts. Do you miss them because you don't spend time on the putting green practicing to make these lengths of putts from all sides of differently sloped holes? If you don't, then you know one of the major reasons why you 3-putt. If you miss the short putts because you don't think you can make them, then you've subverted your intended plan of action and you need to readjust your attitude or focus more on the preparation of the stroke and not the outcome. Only you, with a little help from your internal analyst, can come to grips with the correct solution. But, don't necessarily attribute the cause of your many 3-putts to an either/or factor. Perhaps both enhanced learning and more control of all aspects of your putting routine are called for. Then, and only then, will you increase your chances for success.

Well, that was quite a list, wasn't it? And, you might ask why a writer who apparently believes in the importance of self-confidence would take you down such a path. Surely focusing on the negative is no remediation for poor putting. Certainly not! But, unless you see yourself in some of the scenarios, enough to make you aware of where your putting could use some help, it's doubtful that my discussions, remedies, strategies, and drills will make much sense to you. I didn't write this book to entertain you (although I'm hoping for at least a little smile here and there), I wrote this book to provide you enough rationale for the programming of more successful putting and some specifics that you can use to achieve both my goal and, more importantly, your goal to PUTT BETTER.

FOUR. PUTTING REALLY IS BRAIN SCIENCE

Golf is assuredly a mystifying game. It would seem that if a person has hit [or putted] *a golf ball correctly a thousand times, he should be able to duplicate the performance at will.* Bobby Jones

A golf ball simply cannot find the hole by itself. Even if it could, the ball would never do so willingly, after the hatred and hammering you've heaped on it to get it to the green. Dick Brooks

Did you ever ask yourself "Why can't I putt like I did last week when I shot my best score?" That's the same question that plagues all golfers, amateur and professional alike, and will continue to be as vexing as long as golf is played. On the surface, putting doesn't appear to be a difficult task. You don't have to hit the ball very far, there are no trees or long grass in your path, and you can use almost any putting method to attempt the stroke. Why can't golfers ingrain their putting strokes and replicate their past successes? Consistency is the holy grail of all athletes: "I just want to be consistent and play like I know I'm capable of; the ups and downs drive me crazy." The answers to the above questions can be derived from an understanding of how the brain operates to create what I'll call <u>plans of action</u>. In simple terms, although I hesitate to call brain function simple, the brain has to create every action from scratch. Your putting stroke is not stored in memory, waiting to be unfolded once you reach the green. And, let me clear up one oft-heard fallacy: There is no such thing as muscle memory—memory is solely a brain function. But, how could it be otherwise? Every putt you stroke is different to some degree, even infinitesimally, from every other putt you've ever attempted or will attempt in the future. Getting ready to putt is not like checking a putting stroke out of your mental library. You don't "reach in" and "grab" what you need to attempt the task. It's more complicated than this, and it's just this complexity that leads to putting stroke and putting outcome inconsistencies.

Our brains have the following universal characteristics that factor into the creation of our putting strokes and subsequent outcomes:

* The brain is always on—24/7.

* The brain doesn't automatically care about the outcomes of the plans of action created.

* The brain is an information processor, more likely an image processor, AND a bank for all our memories.

* The brain is the ultimate "multitasker," although there is really no such thing as multitasking because the brain can only process things sequentially, one at a time. But, it can switch so quickly from one task to another to give the appearance of multitasking.

So, you quizzically ask, how does this get us any closer to understanding our putting? Because the brain is always on, that is, constantly picking up cues from the environment, it's understandable that hundreds or thousands or even millions of tiny bits of information may be received by your sense organs at any point in time and subsequently transmitted to the brain. Your sense receptors and brain really "know" more that you consciously know about your environment. Consider the following situation. Two people with equally acute eyesight attend a football game. One turns to the other and says "I can't tell what's going on because I don't know who's got the ball." Both individuals "see" the same the same things but one is a more competent viewer than the other, or as we might say a student of the game. What do you think might happen if you consciously attempted to see all that was going on in the game? Visual overload! And the normal reactions to the recognition of the sensory overload are to start <u>scanning</u> back and forth (like a windshield wiper); <u>chunking</u> by choosing to look here, there, then somewhere else, hoping to make sense of the visual mess; <u>locking in</u> on the quarterback who initially gets the ball; or to give up and say "I don't like this game because I don't understand it." Sometimes you can see too much and this prevents you from seeing clearly. Relate this to the task of reading greens. Is it important to see and process every blade of grass because, if it is, all this will be processed? The result will be visual and cerebral chaos. Yet, the brain wouldn't care and would create a putting line, even though the end-product (from your perspective and desires) would most likely be flawed.

The brain operates on sensory input "somewhat" like a computer (although this is a weak analogy) with a "garbage in, garbage out" principle. As long as you input incorrect or task-irrelevant cues, you're guaranteed to reap the rewards of your neural incompetence. As I stated earlier, the brain doesn't automatically care, doesn't commiserate with you, and won't correct its errors in the future without your intentioned intervention. This reminds me of a previous golfing acquaintance who <u>always</u> missed putts on the low side without any apparent awareness of the pattern, and therefore he made no attempt to remedy his consistent error. If you learn some keys by which to read greens and apply them, then you'll be able to control the quantity and quality of information that the brain uses to establish putting lines. Now you know one of the reasons why you putt badly—poorly constructed plans of action result from faulty input. It doesn't matter whether it's an error of omission (you missed an important cue) or one of commission (you erred in your directional aimline), it's all the same to your cavalier brain.

But there's more to the story. In addition to the brain being an open-ended processor of information, it is also the storehouse of all our memories—good and bad. It's often claimed that human don't forget. Really? "Just the other day I called my good friend . . . um . . . um . . . oh, what's his name." Embarrassingly, your memory lets you down. Yet, a few minutes later, in the middle of an unrelated conversation, your friend's name pops up. The issue is not one of lost memory but one of poor recall. We can also mis-manage our memory. Golfers do this all the time. The following are some examples that will probably hit home. Following a distasteful 3-putt, you blurt out some expletive (*%$#@#). Yet, up to that point you had made several putts from 6 to 8 feet. You make several, miss one, and your memory won't let you forget the missed putt. Conscious or unconscious memory retrieval? Controllable or uncontrollable? As you sit around following your round, you recall the putts you should have made. You shot 85 but missed six makeable putts. In your mind, you really should have shot

79. No mention is made of the chip-in, the long putt that you made, and the two drives that ricocheted off trees into the fairway. In a certain sense, memory can be what you want it to be if you orchestrate the input properly. More on this later.

Think about some really good putts you've made in your lifetime. Now pick one highlight, visualize it, and tell me about it. STOP, don't read any further until you've recalled your putt.

[PAUSE]

You likely rocked your head back a little, rolled your eyes upward as if to "read" out of memory, and the scene of your putt appeared in true color with your playing partners in the picture. Am I close to what you recalled? If so, is the picture vivid and are the people real? Can you tell what you were wearing, what others were wearing, the line the successful putt took, and your emotions when the putt fell in? I expect you answered affirmatively to all or most of these. Now, what do think about your memory when I tell you that there are no pictures stored in your brain, no movies to be screened, and no audio recordings to be played back? If what I'm claiming is true, then where did this elaborate image come from? You know it came from your memory because I asked you to recall this situation. Just as there are no hard copy putting strokes cataloged in the brain, there are no highlight reels of great putts and disastrous putts. And, yet, we can make each come to life as if it just occurred. Sometimes the memory of an event is so vivid and emotion-laden that it races into our consciousness, whether or not we request its presence. I hesitate to mention names but the scenario of Scott Hoch missing the most "unmissable" 2-foot putt in sudden death overtime to lose the 1989 Masters has long ago been entered into the public domain. How often would such a demon likely reappear to you or to any golfer? It's always there to be recalled. Put yourself in Scott's position or in any golfer's position who has failed to close the deal. Would you be able to control the next situation enough to hold back the obvious?

The reason for highlighting the vagaries of memory will be obvious when you hear the whole story how putting plans of action are created. Sensory images are processed in a hierarchical (sequential) step-by-step way, and then are associated with stored past like experiences (but not like adding paint to an oil painting) to create a temporary plan of action. This plan of action is called the **Image-of-achievement** by Dr. Karl Pribram, the noted neuropsychologist and neurosurgeon. Consider how this prominent brain scientist describes how our putting plan of action takes life.

> *A momentary Image-of-Achievement is constructed and continuously updated through a neural holographic process much as is the perceptual image. The Image-of-Achievement is, however, composed of learned anticipations of the force and changes in force required to perform a task. These fields of force exerted on muscle receptors become the parameters of the servomechanisms and are directly (by the thalamus) and indirectly (via the basal ganglia and cerebellum) relayed to the motor cortex, where they are correlated with a fast-time cerebellar computation to predict the outcomes of the next steps of the action. When the course of action becomes reasonably predictable from the trends of prior successful predictions, a terminal Image-of-Achievement can be constituted to serve as a guide for the final phases of the activity.*

Whew! Brain science is tough stuff, isn't it? Please read the quote again, and maybe once more. After a few readings of this really crucial yet complicated description, you hopefully have gained at least a faint glimpse into why I termed putting brain science. I don't want you to be concerned with the finite details of how our overall putting plan evolves, but there are several key points that deserve to be highlighted. The term image-of-achievement lets you know immediately that it's not just an architectural blueprint. It's way more than this! It's a plan that has "how-to-do-it," not merely "what-to-do." Rather than being a static, flat, impersonal plan; it is dynamic, multidimensional, and singularly personal. What all this means is that your putting plan of action is ready to be implemented once it's created, and the degree of achievement will depend on (a) how accurately the plan is constructed, (b) how smoothly the plan is triggered or initiated, (c) what necessary adjustments are made as the plan evolves, and (d) how it plays out to conclusion. The image-of-achievement, as its name implies, is goal- or outcome-oriented, not just action for action's sake. The sensory input, actually perceptual images, must be accurate, much like choosing the correct club for a specified distance. Then, the feel for the necessary direction and distance must be figured into the equation, along with some residue of past experiences, to create the conceptual plan. This describes in a little more detail that motor acts, like putting, are not stored in memory waiting to be elected—they have to be created anew every single time. This is what makes consistency so difficult. All you have to do is slip up on one small part of the planning phase and the outcome will be jeopardized. No two putts are ever alike—similar certainly—but always somewhat different. No putt can be taken for granted because the failure to account for even the slightest nuance can undermine success. And, I'll bet you've have ample evidence of missed putts due to your lack of proper diligence or spotty attitude.

Let's conclude this section by considering just a short sample of the things golfers might do or fail do to affect their putting performance based on what we know about how plans of action are created.

1. If you fail to recognize that the putt is uphill or downhill, the force of the putting stroke will be compromised.

2. If you see a break to the right when the putt actually breaks left, there's no chance of success unless you mis-hit the putt.

3. If you second-guess your read or are uncertain of the read, then this doubt gets figured into the final equation. You can guess the result. Hesitancy leads to defensive putting. But, even with your lack of orchestration, the plan of action will be played out on the green; however not to your satisfaction. Why? Because the putt will undoubtedly come up short of the hole.

4. You hate big breaking left-to-right putts because you never even get them close. As you begin to initiate your putt, what kind of a stroke would most likely occur? Certainly one less confident and not forceful enough to reach the hole, thereby likely leaving your next putt substantially short and low of the hole.

5. You tend to miss short putts. As this anxious feeling gets figured into the image-of-achievement, how rhythmical could you expect your putting stroke to be? Somewhere within the few milliseconds that the plan is being updated, jerkiness finds its way into the mix and the putt is pushed or pulled.

6. You read a putt, you clearly see the line, and you've mastered the speed of the greens all day. Your confident feeling and recent putting successes bias the outcome in your favor because they predispose your memory to positive outcomes.

Strategies to Bias the Image-of-Achievement

The construction of the image-of-achievement is an unconscious process. The brain really doesn't <u>need</u> any conscious assistance in creating the plan of action. In fact, there are plenty of common activities that operate without much, if any, conscious thought (e.g., walking, riding a bicycle, driving a car, and others way too numerous to list). I'd like to set the stage for what's to follow by asking you to go through an imaginary interview for a job or position you'd really like to have. Would you just show up, respond as best you could on the spur of the moment to the questions asked, and let the chips fall where they may? Or, would you try your best to ensure that the employer's decision went your way? If the latter, what are some of the things you'd do to bias the situation in your favor? You'd probably portray your physical appearance in the best way possible. You'd likely anticipate some of the expected questions and plan your responses ahead of time. You'd probably try to impress the prospective employer by displaying your knowledge of the position description and the scope of the company. And, certainly there's an almost limitless number of things you might do, all for the purpose of biasing the interview situation in your favor.

Now let's consider how you might positively bias your putting outcomes by altering the image-of-achievement. Recall that the image-of-achievement is comprised of sensory information linked with memory components from past similar experiences. Where do you think bias might enter into the equation? Consider whether the following make sense to you.

* The quality of the sensory information—**relevance, accuracy, completeness, and vividness**. Rather than inputting a mishmash or hodgepodge of visual cues and leaving it up to the brain to select the best ones, it seems more logical to follow a systematic green reading pattern and only input salient cues. The brain doesn't care about the accuracy of the sensory information; it will act on the data provided. Quality input will increase the chances for a competent output. Optical illusions occur because something in the visual processing system is amiss. I'm reminded of watching a recent golf tournament telecast where a particular putt was missed by all golfers. Nobody could read it correctly. Why not? Does it mean that no golfer could read the putt accurately? That's doubtful, but in this situation the golfers' images-of-achievement were derailed by a lack of the complete picture. Some important visual input was missing or something created a perceptual conflict. There's always the possibility of perceptual inaccuracy. That notwithstanding, is there some way to provide the brain with a vivid sensory "picture"? If you can correctly estimate the amount of break and "see" the putting line from your ball to the hole, then you're providing a huge assist to the brain's filtering out process.

* Your mental approach, attitude, and emotion. Do you think it really matters what feelings you have when you putt? Stan Utley, acknowledged great putter, author, and putting consultant to professional golfers, asserted that the importance of attitude cannot be overlooked. From his own considerable experience as a touring pro, he claimed that he tends to miss well-struck putts when he doubts the outcome. That's his image-of-achievement doing what it's designed to do, namely to add ALL information (perceptual and conceptual, good and bad) into the mix. A good question that might be asked is how a negative attitude works its way into the equation. What kind of past experiences would you expect your memory to resurrect when a doubtful outcome primes your memory? Asked and answered. You already know what a bad putting day feels like and, with a little self-analysis, I bet you could make a list of things you do or fail to do that prolongs the agony. Sit back and think about this for a minute or two. STOP reading.

[PAUSE]

Like all golfers, there are times when we sabotage our own putting successes by poor attitudes and excessive emotion. On the other hand, what does it feel like when your putts are falling? Is your positive attitude merely an outcome based on success or is it possibly a precursor to success? And, are you able to control your emotions because all your putting angels are flying in perfect formation, or does the aeronautical perfection relieve any concerns you might otherwise have? Suffice it to say, you cannot successfully putt anxiously, doubtfully, or emotionally out of control. Your attitude will give you away every time!

   * The degree of automatization of your approach. There's a lot of down-time for golfers between shots and this time will always be filled with thoughts—ALWAYS! Sometimes you control what you think about, and sometimes your mind creates scenarios for you to ponder. I don't suppose you ever worry about making a putt, do you? Do you think a worrisome thought is planned, or is it that a past unsuccessful outcome in a like situation just appeared on your mental "video screen"? Just another rhetorical question. Something more beneficial than worrying about putting outcomes is needed to fill the down times, and this is the process of pre-putt preparation. All golfers need a systematic plan of reading greens, unhurried and yet complete. The movement you see professional golfers make around the green, surveying all the angles, is an orchestrated dance. It is somewhat different among golfers but very exacting within individuals. Some of the dances are quite unique. Jim Furyk makes his read, steps into his putt, then steps back and re-reads his putt. No matter, the important point is that automatization creates a comfort zone, a settled feeling. The approach or stepping into the putt should also be systematized and unhurried. Putting is a tempo-and rhythmically-related motor task, which can be facilitated by a methodical approach. No race is run until the starter's gun sounds. Likewise, no putt should be struck until the final pre-putt preparation is complete and the stroke is initiated by some chosen ritual or strategy (e.g., inhale-exhale-go; forward press-go; look at hole-look back at ball-go). The entire pre-putt routine fills time, and time filled by orchestrating something cannot be filled with anything else. The brain gives us the appearance that it can multitask but, in reality, informational bits can only be processed one at a time. "The devil finds work for idle hands," and a waiting mind

will be quickly filled with the next lurking thought. The brain says, "And that's how we roll."

* The content and quality of your imagery. As you look down the line of your putt, what do you see? Just short grass with a hole cut in it? Or, do you conjure up an image of the putt rolling along your line, eventually falling into the hole, and making that characteristic sound of the ball hitting the bottom of the cup? Recall the elaborate imagery ritual that Jack Nicklaus employed prior to hitting each shot. As good a ball striker as he was, he wasn't satisfied to allow the process to unfold without biasing the outcome with a positive picture of his intentions. I can't imagine that any professional or good amateur golfer fails to create positive images of their intended outcomes. I can assure you that, if they sought assistance from any sport psychologist, successful imagery would be added to their pre-putt repertoire. Perhaps this is just so intuitively factual that we tend to overlook it. But, surely, in your more child-like or pensive moments, you've made putts to win tournaments—tournaments in which you're never likely to play. "See it and you'll believe it." And, see it often enough, and your image-of-achievement will build this positive picture into the outcome. That's biasing the outcome, rather like beating Mother Nature.

* The nature of your self-talking. The things that you say to yourself have much greater impact than you might even imagine. Inner speech is nothing more than expressing thoughts, but it is thoughts that really control actions. ALWAYS! Self-talking can bias performance outcome in either positive or negative ways, depending on the nature of the dialog. "I have no prayers of getting this putt close" creates a very different mind-set (image-of-achievement) than "I have a decent chance of making this or at least getting it close enough to 2-putt." All golfers must be wary of what Erich Harth calls *backward masking*. This happens when a plan of action is masked or suppressed by an unchallenged thought of greater significance. A good example of this happens when you see a putt you don't like and you hear the thought "Don't 3-putt this one." All your planning goes into making a good putt but your negative thought sabotages your good intentions because it adds "noise" to the process. So, what are we to do with these unwanted thoughts? If they occur, then be assured they have some basis. I'll bet you can guess why such thoughts occur and to whom

they occur more frequently? Golfers whose putting competence is shaky, and there's a nasty equation created here. A sense that you're not a good putter leads to the inevitable occurrence of negative thinking about the outcome, and negative thoughts tend to reinforce the feeling of putting incompetence. Although more time will be spent later in the book on the remediation of negative thinking, the basic solutions are to develop more putting competence through practice and by spending more time in planning each putt.

   * <u>Recognize and filter "noise."</u> "Noise" is anything that conflicts or confounds the formation of an image-of-achievement. Examples already mentioned are irrelevant visual cues, faulty attitudes, excessive emotions, negative images, and negative self-talking. "Noise" can occur at any point in the creation of the putting plan of action right up to the execution of the stroke. No matter the timing of the "noise," it must be recognized and its effects must be terminated. The following are some examples of how to deal positively with distractions. You

Reprinted from http://www.funpic.hu. Author unknown.

sense something is wrong with your intended putting line: then step back, start your preparation all over again, re-check your read, step in, and putt. This could occur at any time from when your putting stance is taken until the putting stroke is initiated. I had a couple of tournament best-ball partners who both used to fool me all the time. I'd start to take a step once they initiated their putting stroke only to have them stop mid-stroke to readjust their focus. "Quit fooling me" I'd say, but now I realize that they were the wise ones and I was the fool. You're wise to recognize that's something's amiss but foolish to putt through the confusion, thinking that you can just putt through it. If you feel unsettled over the putt: step back, collect your feelings, perhaps blow off some nervousness with a couple of deep breaths, step in, and putt. If you see yourself miss the putt: step back, check your direction, step in, and putt. What a blessing to recognize that a miss is about to occur; prevent it from happening: step back, re-read, step in, and putt. Better to miss it in your mind than in reality! Did you ever hear of the old Japanese proverb: "Hit your second ball first"? At first blush it doesn't make much sense because you really can't do this—at least, not actually. But in your mind you can. Wouldn't it be great if you could miss your first putt in your mind, make adjustments, and then stroke the actual putt into the hole? Too mystical for you? Dave Pelz reports that a few professional golfers with whom he has worked stand over their putts and see them miss. Then they stroke their actual putts into the hole. This creates for them a positive attitude because they know, like most golfers do, that they most always make their second putts. I call this the Bubba Factor—any golfer can make the putt the second time. Bubba can putt! Any distraction or disruption, real or imaginary (your brain operates the same in either case), is destined to complicate the outcome. My recommendation is to recognize a distraction, deal with it by elimination or acceptance, and re-establish your plan. Never putt through a unchallenged distraction!

To Putt Consciously or Nonconsciously, That is the Question

With what I've described so far, I wouldn't be surprised if you exclaimed "What, putt nonconsciously"? You might be willing to agree that some of the time you appear to putt as if you're out of your mind, but to leave the planning of putts exclusively to the nonconscious might seem more than a little radical. Yet, there are a number of esteemed individuals who support the concept that putting is best performed without a lot on conscious involvement. For example, Bob Rotella claims that *human beings are wired to putt best when the golfer simply sees the target and reacts to it with as little conscious thought as possible.* On what basis does he make such an assertion, you might ask? He admits that he's not sure why our bodies work best this way, but his experiences as a student of the game and as a mental coach to a lot of professional golfers led him to his conclusion. Aaron Baddeley is clearly a proponent of letting the nonconscious brain do most of his putting preparation. He describes his pre-putt preparation as follows: *I'm a little bit different with how I read my greens than regular people* [speaking of his PGA tour colleagues]. *A lot of guys will read, like a ball out of the left lip or three inches . . . . I mean that's too tough for me. I just sort of feel it; I sort of just see like a line going from right to left. So I just sort of try and get out of my way and let the brain figure it out, and then I just try to make the putt.* Aaron's putting statistics reveal him to be one of the best putters on tour [tied for 4th at the time of this writing], so his comments are not to taken lightly. Test this way of putting for yourself. Read the putt as you normally do, but don't pick an aimline. Maybe do as Baddeley does and don't even consciously square your putter to an aimline. See if your nonconscious brain works as well as your normal conscious planning process.

With what I understand about neuroscience, and I must confess that there's so much that escapes me, I have severe reservations about recommending the aforementioned strategy to improve your putting. I tend to support the approach described by Patrick Cohn and Robert Winters, both acclaimed sport psychologists: *If there is one "secret" to great putting, it is this: you must get into each putt with complete attention and concentration, have a specific plan or strategy in mind, believe in your ability, then putt the ball where you want it to go, and accept the results.* This sounds more akin to how I described the construction of the image-of-achievement earlier in this chapter, doesn't it? I believe that you "force" your brain into focused concentration on relevant cues. Why do you think Tiger Woods and some other great putters sometimes create a very narrow focus of attention by cupping their hands on the outside of their eyes or cap brim as they read their putts? Surely it's to limit and direct the brain's processing to consciously chosen cues. No doubt the nonconscious brain can process the visual environment, but at what cost? The nonconscious brain can and will enrich the plan of action by the addition of past memory but with which memory traces? I guess, for me and many others, the question boils down to who's in charge of our putting? Do we control the input and do what we can to bias the image-of-achievement, or do we simply trust that good things will happen. It seems to me that trust has to be based on more than hope.

Experts in human information processing have shed some light on the conscious versus nonconscious approach to putting by highlighting some of the concerns with the nonconscious approach.

1. When the brain creates images-of-achievement without intentional input (rather like Aaron Baddeley's approach to putting), the process leaves no conscious trace. Therefore, how would golfers expect to make changes if the outcome was not successful? I don't mean just the outcome of missing the putt but also why the direction and speed were wrong. If you are an exceptional putter who nearly always makes great putts, then making changes might not be much of a consideration. But, reflect for a moment on golfers like Sergio Garcia and Vijay Singh, who in the 2008 golf season dramatically improved their putting performances. Do you suspect that they made some intended changes, very probably by priming their memory to resurrect more positive images. Much was written about Vijay's protestations about his lack of putting competence, and eventually Vijay proved himself prophetic in demonstrating that he was the good putter he repeatedly claimed he was. Conversely, might Sergio's and Vijay's performances have improved because of enhanced nonconscious processes? This seems doubtful.

2. Nonconscious processing doesn't seem to improve with training or feedback. That's a real shocker, isn't it? This rather echoes the previous point that either you're a good putter or you're not. This fatalistic view is summarily dismissed by Pia Nilsson, mentor to Annika Sorenstam and coach of the Swedish national golf team: *Fact one: anyone with normal coordination can become the best putter in the world. Fact two: great putting can make up for many other faults during a round. But no one putts well day-in and day-out if they don't first believe they are a great putter.* What would it take to improve?

I believe the case has already been made that the answer lies in the competence of the image-of-achievement. If the sensory cues are correct, if the memory attaches the correct feel for the speed of the putt, if the "picture" is of a successful outcome, and nothing interferes with the playing out of the putting scenario, then the outcome will be as good as the external conditions allow. But, what does it take to produce this competence? Deliberate or purposeful practice, not just any "putting the balls around" practice, using sound pre-putt preparation and stroke mechanics, plus a positive attitude—these are essential. This sounds like conscious intentional planning to me.

3. Nonconscious brain functioning, which is normally smooth and orderly, can be disrupted by "noise." In such a case, if the ensuing putt is to have any chance to succeed, the process must be interrupted and some intentional filter or block inserted. Perhaps the most dramatic example of this in golf is the ability of Tiger Woods to stop his swing, which is light years faster that yours and mine, when something untoward occurs in his downswing. If it's really noise from a cameraman, then the solution is more mechanical and Tiger's caddie takes care of it. Let me ask you a question: Which professional golfer has been interrupted more by crowd noise or cameras clicking? And, knowing this, what would a wise golfer do in preparation, just in case it happened? Whether it's outside noise or "noise" created by some doubt or incorrect feeling, then the automatic unfolding of the swing needs to be terminated. The intentioned swing is then rebuilt with the needed change. Does "noise" ever happen during your putting preparation or in mid-stroke? Do you ever feel it and make the necessary adjustments?

4. Can we always trust our brain to provide the best response? Might we better attempt to solve those apparent optical illusions that happen on greens? Sometimes putts break or fail to break because of green conditions that are subtle. I'm not the only one who has experienced this, am I? On a course I previously played regularly, the 14th green looked like it sloped from front to back, but putts sped "uphill" and lagged "downhill." This paradox was solved one day when a member brought out a level and discovered that the green was actually level. This fact plus the direction of the grain made putts roll oppositionally to what was expected. So, put yourself in this situation.

How would you putt this green? You needed to consciously remind yourself that the sloping "back downhill" was not downhill and gather the courage to stroke the putt more forcefully than your brain normally allowed. Conversely, in the other direction, a certain caution was required. This was a kind of error correction that, if forgotten, spelled disaster. Similarly, consider how poorly we usually adapt to greens that are considerably slower than normal. We leave putts short all throughout the round. Why? Because we didn't make the <u>intentional</u> adjustments that needed to be made.

5. For years I putted without any conscious consideration of the <u>fall line</u> of the green. This is the direction a pail of water would drain if you spilled it around the hole, or the putting line crossing the hole that would make the putt a straight one from both the uphill and downhill direction. I was oblivious of the importance of locating the fall line in reading the break of putts. It seems so obvious and elementary that putts are bound to break toward the fall line, not away from the fall line. Where was my unconscious brain all these years? It took conscious awareness to build this into my pre-putt preparation. As you watch golf telecasts on NBC, you'll hear the insightful commentator, Johnny Miller, make several references to the assertion that a particular putt or chip just needs to get started because it is running right down the fall line.

To be fair and balanced, I must admit that there's always the possibility of adding too much information into the putting equation, thereby increasing the chance of confusion and second—guessing. But by following a consistent pattern of reading greens from deciphering the general slope of the putt to the specific putting line, golfers ought to be able to control the sensory input. And, if you limit yourself to just one basic thought as you stand over the ball (e.g., smooth, tempo, rhythm, trust it), the plan of action should unfold smoothly because all the input work has been done. And, to be brutally honest there's really no way of knowing exactly how the brain processes the information it receives. My premises are based on the best information available at this time. I would be remiss if I didn't share with you a very basic rule of behavioral analysis, one you already know and verbalize as "different strokes for different folks." Yes, indeed, the concept of individual differences overrides much of the human behavior we attempt to understand and predict. Aaron Baddeley is not wrong for putting more nonconsciously than I would recommend for most golfers. It works for him, and the proof lies in his putting statistics. Without the benefit of the knowledge of advances made in brain research during the past century, in 1890 William James provided an apt summary to this discussion of how information should be processed for effective putting performance.

> *Whether the attention comes by grace of genius or by dint of will, the longer one does attend to a topic the more mastery of it one has. And the faculty of bringing back a wandering attention, over and over again, is the very root of judgment, character, and will*
> [and I might add competent putting].

FIVE. THE MYSTERY OF READING GREENS

Don't make your stroke until you have the best read you can get. Greg Norman

If I'm breathing heavy while walking on a green, I'm going uphill. If I trip, I'm going downhill. Spec Goldman, Texas amateur golfer

Why term reading greens a mystery? A glance at the dictionary tells us why: A mystery is *anything that arouses curiosity because it is unexplained, inexplicable, or secret.* Well, then, end of chapter? Our experiences reveal a somewhat, although not entirely, different picture because some amongst us are quite good at reading greens. Or, they must be because they make more putts than we do. No matter how good a putting stroke you have, if you don't start the ball on a correct line with the appropriate speed, then only the intervention of divine providence will create a positive outcome. Have you ever been frustrated enough to ask one of your golfing partners to assist you in reading greens, or maybe even read your putts for you? I can recall one occasion when I called for outside help. This occurred soon after I moved to a new course, putting on Bermuda greens for the first time. I'm sure this brings a sinister smile to the faces of those who've had a similar experience. One of my partners was clearly seeing the lines better than I was so I asked him to help me read putts for the remainder of the round. What was the outcome? The best putting day I'd had so far on my new greens. The confidence one has when you believe in the read is truly uplifting. But the problem was that I couldn't bring my green reader along every day I played, so as before I had to count on my own resources to input correct information into my brain. The good news is that we can all improve our green reading capabilities, and the thrust of this chapter is directed at offering you the necessary specifics. A caveat, however, no matter the quality of the information provided, you must heed Bobby Jones' age old advice: *The art* [and science] *of appraising slope and speed—that is, reading a green—can be derived only from experience.*

For the most part Jones' comment rings true, but every now and then a surprise occurs. PGA golfer Patrick Reed (told to *Golfweek*, June 29, 2012) shares just such an anomaly when he talks about his caddie and fiancée: *For some reason, she has a great eye. I don't understand it. She sees a lot of subtlety breaks.* Reed's fiancée doesn't have near the golfing experience he has, but she's able to see the subtle breaks that his eyes miss. Sounds like a "marriage" made in heaven!

Perhaps it might be wise to consider the demands that reading greens place on our information processing system, while at the same time keeping in mind the difficulty of translating the input into successful putts. In more sophisticated psychological terms, putting demands a response to an invariant combination of input events, essentially requiring discrimination (Sorry! I just felt the urge to express this). Select the correct cues and the putt will have a chance; select the incorrect cues and the putt will have no chance. Reading greens is somewhat akin to putting jigsaw puzzles together. As you dump the 1,000 pieces out on the table, you're initially overwhelmed but this soon disappears because you have some learned strategies. You turn the pieces right side up and then look for border pieces. You proceed from general to specific, just as golfers do when they approach the green. Reading greens is the ultimate "multitasking" event because the process of detecting cues, selectively attending to those cues deemed to be important, and categorizing the chosen cues for slope and speed goes on somewhat simultaneously. Just think for a moment what's available for your eyes to see as you scan the green—length of the grass, grain, general slope of the green, slope around the cup, cut of the cup, surface irregularities, and the degree of wetness/dryness of the turf. Walking around the green allows you to <u>feel</u> the slopes and the hardness/softness of the turf. And the strength and direction of the wind highlights something else to consider, especially for us Texas golfers. With this entire palette in front of you, the task is twofold: first, to notice everything (at least globally) and second, to quickly accept or reject most cues. Failure to take into account the degree of slope, for example, spells disaster because the created plan of action misses a key ingredient. Failure to dismiss your prior experiences on a particular green perhaps leads you to underread the slope. This makes the task seem almost impossible, doesn't it? If your make errors of omission, you lose; if you make errors of commission, you lose. Although cues are often referred to as relevant and irrelevant, no cue is irrelevant to the final plan of action but it might be task-damaging. Recall the earlier "garbage in, garbage out" principle of all computer-like operating systems. I'm certain you could easily provide many examples from your own putting experiences where you've sabotaged your putting by perceptual (misreads) or conceptual (negative attitude) errors. The solution to this mystery of reading greens is to become better educated in order to make informed decisions. Or, to phrase it another way, to really attempt to remove the mystery and replace it with understanding.

The solution is, however, not a perfect one. My sense is that you can become a better reader of greens but there's always a chance you'll be fooled by the circumstances. Who would you say are the best green readers? The answer's obvious but watch a professional tour telecast and here's what you're likely to see. On some greens almost all the putts come up short; whereas on others, the reverse occurs. This just demonstrates the difficulty of getting the correct read and then stroking the putt along the intended line. Here's a strange scenario that happened to me recently. On one green I read the break, took into account that the putt "always" breaks right to the Brazos River, yet missed the putt left because the putt did not break as expected. OK, a misread. I allowed my past experiences to color my decision. A few holes later, I encountered another ambiguous situation. This short putt appeared to clearly break right but I decided to strike it firmly to take the break out. The putt missed off the right edge. Not OK, a bad decision. Confusion abounds! What do I do from now on—go with my read of the slope or go with my past experiences? Do you typically encounter ambiguous reads? I think the only solution is to believe your read, which of necessity must match the slope you see with your intended speed. It makes no sense to read a putt two balls left unless you "know" how hard you intend to stroke it. Slope and speed go together. But, your read must also take into account your experiences based on the tendency of a particular green. How much break you add for the tendency is one of the real arts of putting. But, if there's any solace in missing putts because of read errors, remember that golfers more competent than you and I face similar outcomes. Even after many years of experience on the PGA tour, multiple winner K. J. Choi revealed that he still has problems reading greens.

The Process of Reading Greens

Did you ever miss a putt, walk up and tap in the remaining short putt, step back and exclaim "Now I see why my putt broke left" or "Now I can see why I left my first putt short." This rather hopeless after-the-fact revelation was caused by a careless or thoughtless green reading routine, but by then the deed was done. Although no one would likely recommend one routine for all golfers, there seems to be commonalities that deserve your consideration. The best perspective to read putts is initially behind the ball on a line with the hole, shifting your eyes from side to side to decipher the correct ball track to the hole commensurate with the speed you intend to putt. Especially useful is the walk on the <u>low</u> side to the hole to assess the slope that might have been missed from behind. Pay close attention to the read in the last couple of feet because that's where the break will be the greatest. Looking at the putt from too many angles will often confuse you with conflicting information, and your dallying will undoubtedly irritate your partners. If you don't already have a specific routine for reading greens, then you might want to copy Tiger Woods' routine or a variation thereof. Here's how he describes the series of steps he goes through in preparation to putt.

> *I take a general view of the putt while standing behind the ball; walk to the hole, taking a side view of the line to help determine slope; examine the area around the hole; walk back to my ball and crouch behind it, getting the most telling view of speed and break; stand alongside my ball and make two practice strokes; move the putter behind the ball and then shift my feet forward; take two more looks at the line and the hole; stroke the putt.*

Nothing in my mind is more useful than delineating the <u>fall line</u>, the line along which a putt would be dead straight. Dave Pelz has given golfers a great image to use in solving the direction and amount of break question. He suggests that we imagine a clock face overlaid and centered on the hole, with the 12 o'clock to 6 o'clock line running downhill along the fall line. Try to picture a green with a big circle around the cup. Superimpose the numbers 12, 3, 6, 9 on the clockface to represent hours. From this image you can see that all putts will break toward the fall line. For example, putts at 9 o'clock will break left to right; whereas, putts at 3 o'clock will break right to left. And each of these putts will have the most break of any other putt's location. Putts between each quadrant will break more or less depending on their distance or angle from the 12- to 6 o'clock fall line.

If you're good at visualizing, mentally overfill the cup with water and imagine the drain line. If you're not so good at visualizing, walk around the hole (several feet away from it, taking care of others' putting lines), squat down, read the breaks, until you locate the straight putt fall line. Here's a putting truth you can count on—putts will always break toward the fall line. If you don't think you have time for the routine I've generally suggested, then amend your routine as follows: At least always walk to the hole to see and feel the slope and to decipher the fall line. And, if you haven't known about the fall line before, or if you've known about it but haven't implemented it into your pre-putt routine, then begin working with it immediately. Have you ever marveled or been surprised when a big breaking putt was past the hole but then turned back and fell in the hole? What luck, right? Not so, all this indicated that the putt entered the fall line and followed the line right into the hole. Hopefully, this piece of information will consolidate the necessity of reading the fall line—of course, only if you desire to become a better putter.

Reading breaks. Why do most golfers, amateur and professional alike, miss most putts low of the hole? One might think that we golfers would have enough savvy to at least miss half our putts on the high side. But, that's clearly not the case. If you would like to increase your chances of making putts, especially those that have substantial slope, allow me to share Dave Pelz' surprising research findings from over 1,500 amateur and professional golfers. Initially, you might tend not to believe his findings. Even Pelz himself was amazed by his own data. Here's the scoop: Golfers can't see the total <u>visible break</u> of their putts because when they lift their heads they see what appears to be the highest point of the break. However, golfers cannot see the <u>true</u> <u>break</u> of their putts because gravity takes over the instant they strike their putts. They fail to see the initial drop of their putts away from their aimlines because their eyes are looking at the ball. Trust the data—they don't lie. Notwithstanding the nonconscious correction the brain makes to get the read correct, putts are consistently missed on the low side. None of the above has to really matter to us because Pelz has come to our aid and offered a solution. Are you ready? PLAY 2X THE AMOUNT OF BREAK YOU SEE! I know it sounds radical but go to the practice green, choose a breaking putt, read your normal break, double it, and putt.

Reprinted by permission of Finkstrom Licensing International.

Until I read Pelz's *Putting Bible*, my break reading strategy was always a guess but fortunately for me a guess in the right direction. My plan on breaking downhill putts has always been to overread the break and underhit the putt. Picture yourself standing over a big breaking 15-foot downhill sliding putt. What's your concern? Undoubtedly one image you have is seeing the putt fall low of the target line and end up way long and to the side of the hole. Alternatively, and maybe even a worse outcome is that you'll "wimp out" and leave yourself a somewhat shorter but still downhill slider. So how do you normally handle this situation? Is your plan better than playing way more break (2x more) and letting gravity pull the ball down toward the hole? You're feeling nervous, running scared so to speak, and this likely precludes you from making a confident stroke. Rather than fight the inevitable emotion of the moment, if you play more break you can get by with a less confident stroke because gravity will be your friend. I really hope this makes enough sense to you that you'll take my advice (actually Pelz's) and test it out. It really is the solution to reading breaks accurately. If, on the other hand, you don't change the way you read putts, then you'll continue to putt the way you've always putted. I'd really like to see you improve your putting statistics.

Earlier I asserted that the best position from which to read putts is directly behind the hole on a line with the hole. Let's amend the read to encompass what we've just learned from putting on slopes. Once you've figured out the size of the break, say for example a 3-foot break from left to right, establish a mark or target 3 feet left of the pin. Shift your original read position right so now you're on the ball-mark or ball-target line and set up as if this is a straight putt. Actually step to the right to put yourself on the read line. Totally forget about the hole, your aimline is at the selected mark or target. Putt and let gravity take its course.

You've likely heard it said many times that "practice makes perfect." That's really not true; practice makes permanent. Errors can be consolidated as readily as competence. Only perfect practice makes perfect. Use your own experience. Are you a better putter now than you were in the past—last year, 5-10 years ago, or 30-40 years ago? Likely not, unless you practiced meaningfully. If you want to receive blank looks from golfers practicing putts, ask them what they're working on. The following answers would deserve applause: "I'm working on short putts to build my confidence"; "I'm experimenting with the speed needed for uphill and downhill putts"; or "I'm trying to get the feel for the speed of the green." Each of these responses indicates a purpose.

In the hopes of enhancing your competence in reading the breaks of putts, especially deciphering the fall line, thereby raising your confidence level, the following drills are offered.

Trial and Error Drill. This is merely a more systematic version of what you probably already do when you practice putting. Choose a particular spot on the practice green and putt a number of balls to the hole with the intent to make each one or have your misses be 10-17 inches beyond the hole. Notice the break of each and assess your read following the outcome. Did it break more or less than expected? Was it stroked too hard or too softly? Repetition is what enhances learning if, and only if, you get some feedback from the result. Mindless putting without a purpose has no chance of enhancing your putting. Read every practice putt, try to see the line or track, putt with enough speed to get the putt past the hole if it misses, correct your reads and speed, and teach your brain what it needs to bias future putts.

Pick the Correct Line Drill. Zach Johnson, the 2007 Masters champion, sticks a wire hoop into the green about 2 feet in front of his ball on the aimline. The hoop is a miniature version of a croquet gate, a rounded loop of heavy wire with an opening just slightly larger than the diameter of a golf ball. Once he gets the correct read and places the hoop correctly, putts struck with the proper speed will go in or be very close. He putts 10 putts before he moves to another location and repeats the process. If you like this drill, purchase 2 feet of plastic-coated wire and bend it around a piece of 2" PVC pipe or some other round object about 2 inches in diameter (golf ball diameter is a little less than 1 3/4 inches). The ends of the hoop can then be cut to length. You can see the video of Zach practicing with the hoop by accessing *Zach Johnson putting drill* on the web. The hoop is also very useful for practicing short putts with the hoop placed close to the hole.

Last 3 Feet Drill. As you're practicing reading breaks, walk up close to the hole and scrutinize the last 3 feet. Those well-struck putts that come agonizingly close to going in might have a better result if the break around the hole was read in conjunction with the overall break.

My suggestion is during practice and during actual play put on your "binoculars" around the hole. It takes so little time and may pay huge rewards.

Find the Fall Line Drill. Earlier in this chapter I described the clock face metaphor for reading putts according to the fall line. It's a lot easier to physically practice locating the fall line than it is to mentally find it, at least at the onset. Place a number of balls around a hole that has some apparent break. Putt each of them noticing the break. When you find the putts that have no break, figure out which is uphill and which is downhill. That's the easy part. Mentally superimpose the clock face on the hole and practice putting, first from 3-5 feet, then from 6-10 feet. Putting farthest away from the fall line (3- and 9 o'clock) will break more than putts close to the fall line (1- and 7 o'clock).

Hills and Valleys Drill. Flat putts or sloping putts do not pose the problems that rapid changes in elevation cause. Picture a 20-foot putt rising uphill for the first 12 feet, flattening out for 3 feet, and then gradually moving down to the hole for the last 5 feet. Break the putt into segments as if each segment was the actual putt. Read back from the hole to the exit point from the plateau down to the hole (keeping in mind the fall line) and create the feel for slope and distance; then read from the entry point onto the plateau across to the exit point and again create the feel for distance; and then go the ball, read the break, and feel the distance to the entry point of the plateau. Putt the ball with enough speed to climb the hill, traverse the plateau, and slowly move down to the hole. Essentially, I hope you can visualize three separate reads with one aimline. Once the reads are translated into the correct aimline, the only concern is getting the right speed. Locate some undulating putts if you can find them and practice the separate reads concept. If not, keep the idea in mind when you encounter such putts.

2x the Break Drill. I suspect you still might not be convinced that you need to double your read, especially on big breaking putts. The proof will be in testing it out for yourself with one caveat however. You must select and commit to an aimline, perhaps by marking a line on the ball and aiming it at the target (NOT the hole but some selected spot on the green that you estimate is far enough removed from the hole to allow for the putt's break). This is to prevent your brain from making a seemingly necessary adjustment because your normal read is typically so short of the amount of break required. Did you ever make a putt when at impact you felt you pulled or pushed it? Did you chalk it up to a lucky mis-hit? Perhaps you never considered that your brain "knew" more than you did. What I mean is that you provided the accurate visual input, felt confident over the putt because of positive past similar occurrences, and then the brain created a competent image-of-achievement. This can happen, and Dave Pelz has documented just such consciously unplanned adjustments. There's a "game" our brain plays on us at times, and I feel certain you'll recognize the following incidents or ones similar. Just the other day I lined up my tee shot to a target on the right side of the fairway with out of bounds right, with the intention to draw the ball left into the fairway. But, on the downswing, there must have been some automatic brain override because I pulled the ball way left of my intended target. Did my brain know something I didn't know? Had I nonconsciously programmed something into the swing? On other occasions I've pulled or pushed a putt off my intended aimline only to be surprised to see the putt break back into the hole (not often, mind you, but occasionally). Did my brain know something I didn't know? As much as I'm a proponent of consciously orchestrating my own destiny, the brain does make unplanned adjustments (not for it but for me), once again reinforcing the mystery of neuroscience. I repeat my earlier assertion: Putting <u>really</u> is brain science!

You'll notice that each of the above drills addresses a particular aspect of reading putts. Many golfers find practicing their putting to be quite boring because it doesn't seem to have the intuitive appeal of hitting full shots. However, putting practice will pay much greater dividends than beating drivers on the range, if practice is well planned. Hopefully the above drills with their varied purposes will add some interest to your putting practice. I can guarantee that purposeful putting practice will improve your putting. Test this out for 2-3 weeks of serious practice and see whether I'm correct.

Reading grain. Bermuda greens pose a much greater problem for golfers than do bent greens. Grain influences both the speed and break of putts. Obviously down-grain putts roll faster than into-the-grain putts. Cross-grain also impacts the break of putts. Fortunately, grain is not nearly as important as slope and speed. But that's little consolation to a golfer whose putt comes to an abrupt halt a mere partial roll short of the hole because of the retarding influence of grain. A miss is a miss! So it's worth spending a little time to help you identify the grain of greens. Grass tends to grow down slopes where water runs off and leans toward the sunny exposure. Down-grain direction tends to look shiny, sometimes whitish in color. Up-grain direction tends to be darker. The direction the grass leans is readily assessed on some greens by reading your putt's line and then turning your head to see the different shading in the other direction. Whiter is faster, darker is slower. Another way to assess grain direction is to look how the cup is cut. If one side is cut more sharply than the other, then the grain runs to the hole from the "shaggier" side to the sharply cut side. There are more important demands of reading greens than deciphering grain, but I wouldn't recommend overlooking grain if the putt is directly uphill or downhill, particularly a downhill slider.

Reading speed. Now we've reached the "real" mystery of reading greens, namely how to judge the force required to stroke the ball the required distance. And, what is the required distance? Although there are putters like Jack Nicklaus who believed in rolling the putt just over the front lip of the hole, research has shown that the optimum putting speed carries the ball a few inches inches past the hole if it misses. If we all could do this we would save ourselves the anguish of leaving putts dead in the hole but short, or having putts break just off the hole for lack of speed. Even if we exceed the 10-17 inch beyond-the-hole rule by a foot or so, that's probably better than coming up short. Most 3-footers can be made, even by less accomplished golfers. So we have a plan and the logic seems sound, but applying the logic is a whole other matter. Although reading slopes and lines is not easy, that challenge pales in comparison to achieving distance control.

The question that we need to pursue at this point is how to create the plan of action (recall the image-of-achievement concept described in an earlier chapter) that will encompass the feel needed to give a putt a decent chance of arriving at its planned destination. Some have suggested that putting is an nonconscious act and that speed will take care of itself if the read is correct and your attitude is positive. As

I'm spending more time writing this book and less time playing golf, my infrequent presence on the links is being "rewarded" with higher scores. Not surprisingly, my scores suffer due to more frequent 3-putts and less success than normal even from makeable ranges. Proper speed isn't just happening for me and I'm quite certain it's also not just happening for you. Have you noticed that the first part of the game to leave you after an absence is the short game? For you northern folks, you probably even surprise yourself on your first spring outings how well you're hitting the ball. But chipping and putting is a different matter, isn't it? Clearly it takes more that trust in the nonconscious to return to your normal level of skill even though you've stored many thousands of putting successes in your memory. We expect these decrements and we know, at least in part, how to remedy them. But, for those who don't have any answers, Lee Trevino offers the solution: *There is no such thing as a natural touch. Touch is created* [or recreated] *by hitting millions of golf balls.* Millions!

Poor distance control leads to 3-putts and psychologically draining and anxiety compounding second putts. I'm sure you've heard the golf TV commentator saying: "He can't keep leaving himself so far from the hole and expect his putting to keep bailing him out." Rather than relying on the brain to "figure out" the required distances, it seems much wiser to take a more proactive approach and "teach" the brain to match distance with feel. This is another way in which you can bias the image-of-achievement to be more competent. Certainly the plan of action strives for competence and, even though its creation is a nonconscious event, conscious and purposeful practice can improve the end result. Have you ever had the experience of playing on really slow greens and leaving your putts short all day? Have you ever played on really fast greens and consistently left your putts long all day? Of course you have, as have millions of other golfers worldwide. Jeff Ritter, a PGA professional, offers a way or remediating these situations. Once you realize that you have poor distance control, here's a way of "fooling the brain" (really biasing the brain to create a more competent plan). On slow greens step back from the ball on the target line and take 2-3 rehearsal strokes that you feel would be necessary to get the ball 10-17 inches past the hole. Quickly step up to ball and putt with that rehearsed feel in mind. Conversely, on fast greens step towards the hole on the target line and take 2-3 rehearsal strokes. Step back to the ball and putt. You might wonder about the validity and utility of this chicanery. Purists might claim you shouldn't have to stoop to such tactics, and advocates of nonconscious putting might argue that the brain really knows best and can't be fooled. The brain needs input to operate and biasing the process by more and less forceful rehearsal swings will work in your favor IF you believe more in the feel that you've generated and less in your visuals. As a comical aside, I just think about how many times our brains undermine our performance because we utter an apparent reminder such as, "Don't leave it short." The brain hears the most significant part of the message "leave it short," shrugs its cerebral shoulders, and says "I can and will do this for you but I don't know why you want this result, but it's your plan." As golfers we need to be cautious what input we create or "allow' to be created because the brain will always operate on its input. In the case of repeated poor distance control, some preparatory adjustments need to be made or you'll berate yourself once the round is over for failing to adjust: "I left every putt short all day!" That's a sad indictment, wouldn't you agree?

Consider the truth and importance of one of Dave Pelz's dictums: *It is better for golfers to know the distance of their putt rather than guess it.* Now it's time to offer some practice and pre-round drills that address distance control—the main reason for poor putting.

Make Solid Contact Drill. You'll never develop a consistent feel or touch for distance unless you always make solid contact with the ball. Practice making solid contact with this suggestion from Peter Krause (*Golf Magazine*, February 2008). Set a gate of two tees ½ inch outside the heel and toe of your putter. With a ball in the middle of the gate, practice putting to another tee 20 feet away. Repeat with a distance of 30 feet. These are common distances of first putts you'll normally find on the course (unless you're a superb iron player). Once you can putt without touching either tee you're not pushing or pulling, nor contacting the ball on the toe or heel of the putter.

Consistent Stroke Drill. If you come up short on one putt and hammer the next putt long, this drill will help you build stroke consistency. Good putters maintain the same <u>tempo</u> throughout the stroke, NOT a nice slow backstroke and a jabbed and hurried forward stroke. A good way of finding your personal comfortable tempo (1-back, 2-forward) and ingraining it is with a metronome. There are several free apps that are available to be downloaded to your smart phone or tablet. For short putts, especially, try 50 beats per minute and see what you think. Experiment. Good putters also equalize the length of the backstroke and forward stroke. With a ball just outside your putting plane (using it as a reference point), practice several even tempo and equal distance strokes. Length of stroke forward and back can be measured with tees. Practice putting balls in succession trying to create as close a grouping as possible. Choose different distances in order to groove a feel for each distance. You don't have to practice all distances because your brain is capable of adjusting your putting stroke, based on some baseline distances. You see this happening in basketball, for example, when a shooter makes shots when he or she is pushed away from their favorite spot on the floor.

Duplicate Strokes Drill. Use 3-5 balls. Stroke the first putt to any random distance. Try to replicate this stroke with the remaining balls. Vary this drill by putting to a tee at different measured distances. Try some putts uphill, downhill, and sidehill.

17 Inch Beyond Drill. Use 3 balls. Place one tee 3 feet from the hole and a second 17 inches beyond the first. Try to leave no putts short of the first tee and none longer than the second tee. Repeat the drill with the following distances: 8, 12, 15, 20 feet.

Clock Drill. Place 4 balls around the hole, each 3 feet from the hole. Make all putts then move the balls to 4 feet. Continue adding 1 foot as long as you make all four. If you miss, repeat the 4 at the distance you missed. Don't forget to read each putt and locate the fall line.

Ladder Drill. Place tees at 3, 5, 7, 9, 12, 15 feet from the pin (maybe just the first three or four distances to start). Make the first and continue to putt until you miss. If you miss return to the beginning and start over. The task is to see how far up the ladder you can climb. For a variation, make two putts before you move up, and then maybe three putts. All putts need to go past the hole if missed. Tough!

Plus Minus Drill. Place a tee 17 inches behind the hole. Lay down a line of 5 balls perpendicular to and 5 feet from the hole. Score each putt as follows: +1 for a make, -1 for a putt short of the hole or longer than 17 inches, 0 for a miss past the hole but within the 17 inches. Repeat and keep your scores. Try the drill from different distances.

Triangle Drilll. This is Pelz's favorite distance control drill so it comes highly recommended. Choose three holes in proximity to each other that will form a triangle. Measure the distance between a pairs of holes. It's better to know your distances than guess them. Use 3 balls and putt all three sides of the triangle in a clockwise direction, then in a counterclockwise direction. Keep repeating.

Putt to a Tee, Coin, or Phony Hole Drill. Pre-round drill. The putting green is often crowded before tee times so forget the hole. Set one tee or coin at your ball and the other 20 feet away and putt to it with 2-3 balls. Putt in the reverse direction. You can obtain a phony hole from most restaurants or adult beverage watering holes because their coasters are reasonable facsimiles of the cup size. I carry a Stella Artois coaster in my golf bag. This can be tossed down anywhere at either a measured or random distance.

Putt to the Fringe Drill. Pre-round drill. Use 2-3 balls. The intent is for the putt to reach the fringe without rolling off the green. Measured or random distances can be used. If possible, practice some putts both uphill and downhill.

Graduated Backstroke Drill. Pre-round drill. Because the distance a putted ball travels is, or really should be, determined by the length of the backstroke, let's develop a formula for distance control. To determine the speed of the greens on any given day at any course, place a tee 6 inches behind the ball just slightly off the aimline of a flat putt. Take the putter back to the tee, swing forward 6 inches and measure how far the ball travels. Repeat several times. Next move the tee back to 1 foot and repeat the putting sequence. Lock these distances into memory as they'll be very useful out on the course, especially if the course is new to you. Make some similar putting attempts on an upslope and a downslope, and again take note of the distances. A variation of this drill (from Ted Sheftic, *Golf Magazine*,

October 2008) is to take the putter back to the inside of your back foot, putt, and pace off the distance. Next take your hands back to the outside of your back toe and measure the distance. When you play you'll have a feel for two different distances that can be modified for the slope. Another variation was aired on the recent Masters (2014) TV coverage. On very fast greens, concentrate on the distance your top thumb moves rather than on the movement of your putterhead.

Eyes Closed Drill. Certainly short putts are missed when the putterhead pushes or pulls the ball off the target line, but perhaps more often failure results because a weakly hit putt veers off line due to the break and lack of speed. I remind you of the 10-17-inch past the hole rule which, if implemented, will eliminate the short putt from breaking off the hole. Putt several short putts hard enough for the misses to go past the hole, then close your eyes and attempt to replicate the firm putting stroke. Open your eyes when your stroke has completed. Three benefits will accrue. First, you'll develop the feel for the force needed to putt the ball firmly along the target line. Second, you'll have fewer putts breaking off the hole and missing. And, third, by not lifting your head because there's nothing to see with your eyes closed, you'll avoid coming out of the putt.

Long Putts Drill. I played on a course where the 18th green is over 50 yards in depth and where a strong wind is often blowing in your face or at your back. You can imagine that many iron shots end up mighty short of a pin stuck way in the back of the green with the into-the-wind condition and way long of a short pin in the down-wind condition. How do you give yourself an opportunity to 2-putt from distances of 100 feet or better? My suggestion is to make your practice strokes while looking at the hole, even if you're not accustomed to making practice strokes at all. Also, opening your stance will allow for a less restricted putting stroke. There's research to show that golfers who even look at the hole while putting make more long putts. This drill gives you two strategies to try when you're practicing. The former doesn't really require any real change to your pre-putting routine, but the latter needs some practice attempts to convince yourself that you are capable of striking the ball solidly while looking at the target. Missing the ball altogether might be too embarrassing for you to handle. It certainly would be with the scoundrels I play with.

Create a Putting Gauge Drill. One of the greatest problems with judging the speed of particular distances is that greens have slopes. So even if you have created a good feel for a 30-foot putt, a mental equation needs to be calculated to adjust for the slope. Mike LaBauve (*Golf Magazine*, May 2009) has created an adjustment gauge that you might try. Because 30 feet (10 paces) is a common first putt distance, practice this distance until you are able to reasonably recreate this feel. Lock in the length of stroke and tempo to provide an anchor. Use the following chart to make adjustments for slope.

Length	Slope	Change
5 paces	Uphill	None
5 paces	Downhill	1/4 force
10 paces	Uphill	1 1/2 force
10 paces	Downhill	3/4 force
15 paces	Uphill	2x force
15 paces	Downhill	None

Try this adjustment and see how well it works for the course(s) you play regularly. And, when you're going to play a new course, get your 10-pace stroke down pre-game and use the adjustment gauge.

There are two additional perspectives on green reading I want to bring to your attention. The first comes from Dave Pelz, the short game guru. At the time of this writing he is deeply immersed in a *learning to read greens project*. He expects to have completed his research and testing by mid-2012. He publishes a regular column in *Golf Magazine* so be on the lookout for his guidelines. I can promise you some good suggestions.

The second perspective is a "revolutionary" method of reading greens, one that flies in the face of the assertion made by one of the great putters and putting teachers, Dave Stockton, who claimed that there is no scientific way to determine break. Enter Mark Sweeney, the creator of AimPoint (see aimpoint.com golf), the Emmy Award-winning method of replacing aiming by feel or touch with mathematics, physics, and three-dimensional geometry. So, again I say, putting

REALLY is brain science. Perhaps you've already seen AimPoint in operation on the Golf Channel during tournament telecasts. The line on the green from ball to hole, showing the break of the putt, is not created by some black art but by AimPoint specifications. If you can't read breaks you can't putt, and if you can't control speed you can't putt. So, somewhat akin to Pelz, Sweeney's method is based on putting a ball at a speed that would propel the ball 10 inches past the hole if missed. Speed control is paramount and previous drills have been described for you to attain proficiency in putting certain distances, with corrections for slope.

The first step is to find the "zero line," which previously has been called the fall line—same thing. Sweeney advocates reading the slope first, not reading the aimline from behind the ball. Once you've become attuned to prioritize the search for this line along which a putt would be straight and spent time on the practice green with drills to develop your competence, the time involved will become very minimal (Sweeney claims this will take 5 seconds). The next step is to figure out how far the ball is from the hole—pace it off. Recall the clock face metaphor with its 90 degree right angles between 12 and 3, 3 and 6, 6 and 9, and 9 and 12. Within one these quadrants, estimate the ball-to-hole angle from the zero line. If half way, the angle would be 45 degrees. Next estimate the stimp (the speed of the greens)—8 (slow), 10 (medium), or 12 (fast). Often this can be determined by asking at the pro shop or gained from the starter. This takes almost no time. Then, make an assessment of the slope—flat (1%) to severe (4%).

Let's set up an example. The distance is 13.5 feet, the ball angle is 15 degrees, and the slope is 2%. What is the amount of break? Of course you don't know because you don't have the AimPoint charts. If you had them in front of you, the exact amount of break would be listed without any guessing on your part. AimPoint clinics are offered around the country for around $200 (2012). Fundamentals are taught and practiced, and participants leave with putting charts. Mobile apps are also available for both Apple and android, and break amounts are shown in both English and metric values. You might want to check this out with keywords AimPoint and/or AimCharts.

Basic Principles, Truths, and Rules of Putting

In no special order, the following summarize some basics to guide your putting to further help you solve the mystery that you face every time you pick your putter up.

1. Remember the 2x rule in order to counteract the tendency that ALL golfers have of underreading the break of their putts

2. Almost every putt breaks—there are extremely few straight putts.

3. Nearly <u>all</u> golfers tend to miss putts on the low side.

4. Forget the "pro" side and the "amateur" side. In putting there are no moral victories; a miss is a miss and adds one additional stroke to your score.

5. Slope is the most important determinant of break.

6. Speed of the stroked putt determines the amount of break. Fast putts break less than slow putts. That explains why putts that look good 1 foot from the hole tend to slide off the edges of the hole; putts are traveling slower near the hole.

7. Downhill putts break more than uphill putts.

8. Putts ALWAYS break toward the fall line. If you become proficient at reading fall lines, then you're well on your way to unraveling the mystery of putting.

9. Putts that fall short of the hole never go in (Have you noticed this?). Work on the 10-17-inch rule.

10. Putting without a proper read and purpose is like shooting a rifle without sighting the target. Think about this!

11. Putt with the intent of making every putt (and I might add every chip). Why build the proverbial "inside-3-foot-circle" plan

of action into your intention? Forget the "get it close" rule. Really, I don't know how to assist the brain in creating the 3-foot-circle image-of-achievement? Miss it long, miss it short, miss it to the right, miss it to the left? Can you picture your brain's response? "What! . . . . Is your intention to totally confuse me? Do you want to make this putt or not?" (Your brain does talk to you, doesn't it?)

12. Slope and speed are interrelated components of reading greens. Because there are many paths the putted ball can take into the cup, the correct one is the one that matches line with speed.

13. When putting straight up a slope that flattens before the hole, the ball will tend to break right if your putt is left of the fall line to start and left if your ball is right to start.

14. Don't make a habit of second guessing your read. Normally that will destroy your confidence. But, don't hesitate on rare occasions to step back and reread your putt when you feel something's not right.

15. Use your putting routine and green reading keys to come quickly to a decision. Trust your read and putt confidently.

16. Watch others when they putt, see how much break they play in relation to how hard they stroke the putt. Pay particular attention to the length of others' backstrokes and assess if they pushed or pulled their putts. Caution! If in doubt go with your read, and remember that all golfers have particular idiosyncracies.

SIX. DANGER LURKS ON THE SHORT GRASS

Golf inflicts more pain than any other sport. If you're the sort of person whose self-worth is tied up in how you play, golf will cut you to the core of who you are. Jim Loehr, sport psychologist

On the putting green the mind can be a grave source of trouble. Begin to dislike the look of a putt, and the chances of holing it at once become less. Joyce Wethered, great British golfer

As has already been explained earlier, putting accounts for a major proportion of our golf scores. And, when things go askew on the greens, the success we desire is doomed. Golfers have fragile egos because there are so many negative putting incidents or episodes that they potentially face. So many 3-putts, so many blown short putts, so many lip-outs, etc., etc., etc. And, there always seems to be pressure to make a putt, whether it's to keep a round going, to secure or salvage a good round, or even to win a match or tournament. Putting is what keeps golfers playing the game or what drives them from it. Even at the very top level of golf, professionals give up competitive golf because they are no longer willing or able to deal with the frustrations of putters gone astray. The gulf between that "what was" and "what is" is too wide and cannot be broached. This chapter has a two-fold purpose: to explain the common putting dangers, and to offer solutions. We'll deal with slumps, missed short putts, consistent misses, inconsistent outcomes, getting on the bogey train, yips, and the mismatch between practice and on-course putting performances.

Putting Slumps

All human behavior is distributed normally. By this I mean that there are a few really great putting days and a few really ugly putting days, but most putting days fall in between these two extremes. For good putters the performance curve has more of a north/south direction, like a rounded mountain with steep inclines on both sides. There's little variation in putting performance for good putters, yet they still have their not so good and extremely good putting days. For poor putters the performance curve takes on more of a flattened east/west direction, like a squashed rounded hill with shallow inclines. Poor putters have wider putting performance variations, yet they still have really bad and good days. But, what we're addressing here is the prolonged miring of your putting performance in the poor end of the curve. I mean, hole after hole, round after round, being very frustrated with your putting.

Why does this happen, and can it be remedied? Clearly, the explanation resides in you, the golfer, not in outside factors. Accept that you are causing the problem. Slumps start very innocuously with a bad putting day, and all golfers experience them. It is your response to the problem that exacerbates the situation. If you let it pass without excessive concern, then perhaps it's just one of those days—part of the normal distribution of putting performance. Did you ever play great one day and then play horribly the very next day? Or, have a great front nine but foul up on the back nine? This only happens to you, right? The best professional golfers don't shoot 63 one day and then shoot 72 the next, do they? The point I'm making here is that putting is a difficult task that's bound to lead to inevitable score variations—some very large. But, we're dealing here with consistently poor putting. Perhaps it might be helpful to look at the sport of baseball because it's rife with batting slumps, which can be chronicled by a numerical score. A .300 hitter goes 1 for 15 in his last 5 games, that's .067. Naturally he's unhappy so something must be done to remedy the situation because "that's just not me." Something's wrong, so let's fix it! So the baseball player starts tinkering with his swing—widening or narrowing his stance, taking more or fewer practice swings, opening or closing his stance, altering his head position, etc. And, guess where all this leads? You're correct! Further away from the fundamentals that made him a .300 hitter. Let's return to the golfer's world. It's more difficult to operationalize putting failures, that is unless you keep track of your performance (missed short putts, 3-putts, etc.), but your gut reaction provides enough factual data that your putting is letting you down. What is your remedy? To change your putting grip or stance, to move the ball forward or backward in your stance, to putt quicker or slower, to question your reads, or to change putters? Does this work? Of course not likely because you're grasping at straws, making changes when you don't know the cause(s) of your putting decline. All this will do is further the downward spiral, certainly not something you intend or want. And I must ask an even larger question: When you're putting badly, what's your attitude like? How confident are you in making your putts? These are rhetorical questions that need no answers because they're universally intuitive. So put together random and unsystematic mechanical changes with an utter lack of confidence and you have the perfect equation for a continued slump. You don't know how to putt and you have no positive feeling about the outcome, really it's really even worse than this: You KNOW the next putt isn't going in the hole.

Before I offer you any solutions, I want to remind you of the points covered earlier in the chapter dealing with factors that limit putting success. If putting slumps are a particular issue for you, perhaps you might go back and reread this section before you proceed any further. There's one reality check I need to highlight, and that's putting statistics from the best putters in the world (90% success from 3 feet, 50% from 6 feet, 30% from 9 feet, 20% from 12 feet, 10% from 20 feet, and 5% from 30 feet). You and I are not likely going to be this successful, so keep your expectations in the real world. (Unless, of course, you harness the essence contained in this book).

Slump busting strategies center around mechanics, pre-putt routines, and confidence. You ought not to make changes in any of the above without first ensuring which one is to blame. Fiddling with mechanics will soon get you to the point of slump consolidation. If you suspect that your fundamentals are lacking, then you likely need some outside assistance to help you. Perhaps you've moved the ball in your stance relative to your normal sightline or any number of things. Changes may have been made so gradually over time that they haven't been really noticeable until you're putting performance reached the "I can't stand it anymore" stage. I caution you to be very careful about making random changes to assuage your desperation because incorrect changes will have dire and compounding consequences.

More likely, slumps are not caused by physical factors. Rather they are attributed more often to your attitude and behavior. Chances are you're irritated or frustrated over your recent ineptitude, and this shows in your green reading, pre-putt preparation, and confidence. It's difficult to slow down enough to commit yourself to a systematic preparation to putt when you feel like the outcome is not going to be positive. Why go through all the preparation and then miss the putt? Why not give the line a casual glance and get it over with? Does this sound like a recipe for success? Let me share a catchy but very useful three-part strategy that I know will help any golfer dig out of a putting slump. A fellow sport psychologist friend of mine, David Cook, has created a plan that he has utilized in his work with amateur and professional golfers—called **See it . . . Feel it . . . Trust it**. If you apply this strategy to your practice and on-course putting, I believe you'll begin to find your way out of your putting woes. The strategy is explained in a later section dealing with imagery strategies and drills.

The final point to highlight in relieving slumping putting performance is to come to grips with the insidious nature of basing your putting confidence solely on outcomes. As you may recall from your reading of previous chapters, there are many reasons why putts miss—even perfectly read and wonderfully struck putts. As your slumping performance degrades further and further, the normal human reaction is to focus more on outcomes, and in this case negative outcomes. Would you even believe that you could improve your performance by focusing and ruminating about the inevitable failures? Sit back and think for a moment . . . what's all that you can do? Make your best preparation and execute a confident putting stroke. What happens after the ball leaves your putter just happens. At this point the outcome is out of your control. I remind you again that, except for short putts, most putts are missed—it's not even a 50:50 proposition. If you want to increase your chances for putting success, your focus has to be on the physical and mental aspects of preparation. Failure makes you anxious—you want to do things quickly. But, doing things quickly interferes or overrides systematic green reading, seeing aimlines, and executing smooth putting strokes. Your focus must be on preparation and execution, not outcome. So, how do you start to dig yourself out of putting slumps? Go to the putting green and consolidate your fundamentals—See it . . . Feel it . . . and Trust it. When this becomes your focus, you're on your way to better putting.

Missed Short Putts

Short putts are missed because it is not physically possible to make the little ball travel over undulating ground for three or four feet with any degree of regularity. Walter Hagen

Let me begin by asking some pertinent questions to lay the groundwork to understand and remedy this putting problem.

Why are short putts the most feared?

Why are short bogey putts so much easier to make than short par putts?

Why are short par putts so much easier to make than short birdie putts?

Why do we beg for "gimme" putts?

Why do we give our playing partners short putts?

Why is it that we can successfully "rake in" a short putt (maybe even 3 or 4 feet) following a missed first or second putt?

Why is it we can walk up to a previously missed putt and, without much if any preparation, stroke the short putt into the hole?

Surely you recognize some, if not all, of these normal occurrences. They don't seem to make a lot of sense, do they? Short putts are made with great regularity. Theoretically (but realistically?) a 3-foot putt is a 3-footer no matter if it's for eagle or double-bogey. Short putts are so easy that we don't even bother to ask our partners to putt them. In fact they're so easy they can be made without giving much attention to them. Why do we miss them? And, why do the best golfers in the world miss them, sometimes to lose tournaments?

There's a certain expectancy that surrounds short putts that doesn't occur with longer putts. Golfers expect to make their short putts and their playing partners are also counting on them to make the short ones. This high outcome expectation creates a complicating mindset to the putting process because it places the focus on the outcome not the preparation. And, if you've played much golf, you recognize a bit of the unsettled feelings you have over putts that should be automatic. Scott Peck claims that our *idolatry of score* constitutes a real trap. You miss a putt you "should" have made ("I could make that putt with my eyes closed"), and automatically the score calculator in your mind starts whirring. Your score is ruined! This missed putt spells doom for the rest of the round! Just think, if you can tap in short putts—backhand even—why are you concerned about their difficulty? We're back to a lack of trust, created by doubts of the outcome. Why? Because doubt adds "noise" to the system, and recall how noise impacts the plan of action. Forget about the outcome, and dismiss the supposed fact that short putts are automatic. Any length putt can be missed for all kinds of reasons. What you want to do is focus on what you can control, and these are preparation and trust.

For those of you who feel or claim that you just can't putt, you create a self-fulfilling prophecy. The thought and emotion of a missed short putt roll around in your brain and become part of your plan of action the next time a short putt pops up. Would you recommend to others that they should carry over their negative thoughts and feelings to the next situation? Would you learn this concept at Dave Pelz, David Leadbetter, Jim McLean, Hank Haney, Jim Flick, or Rick Smith golf schools? Of course not, that would be stupid! AHA! Maybe a breakthrough moment. Nobody would recommend this strategy to others but it's acceptable for yourself? It's important that a missed putt only add one stroke to your score (0.01% of your score if you shoot 90) and not create a cumulative effect by undermining the trust on subsequent putts. It serves no positive purpose to excuse a missed putt by exclaiming "I just can't putt." This only adds fuel to the fire!

Try the following drills to assist you in focusing on squaring the putterface to the target line and to prove to yourself that you don't have to be perfect to make a putt.

Four Corners Drill. Credited to David Frost, PGA tour player. Realize the cup is almost three golf balls wide, and teach yourself that you don't have to hit the hole dead center to make the putt. Practice putting straight 3-foot putts at the front left and right edges. See how far out you can stroke the putt and still make it. Likewise, practice putting just over the front lip and also to the back edge of the cup. What you'll realize that there's a lot of cup for you to putt into, and your confidence will rise Don't be automatic in practice—pick your line and trust your stroke. Move around the hole, add some distance, try some left-and right-breaking putts. Also, try placing a flat ball marker instead of a ball about 3 feet from the cup and make putting strokes in slow motion. This should allow you to attend more closely to the reason(s) for your errors. More specifically, it will enable you to feel the integration of hands, arms, shoulders, etc. to identify any swaying, pushing, and pulling actions. This latter technique is an adaptation of a daily drill used by Russian tennis teachers to develop players into world class performers such as Marat Safin and a host of others. If you'll take these practice green experiences to the course, your short putt misses should decline.

Prevent Pulls and Pushes Drill. Keith Lyford (*Golf Magazine*, March 2011) tells that 75% of all recreational golfers cut across the target line with their putters, resulting in both pulled and pushed putts. Certainly some short putts are stroked too firmly and bounce out of the back of the cup and others are stroked cautiously and end up short, but most short putts are missed right or left. Try this. From about a foot away from the cup, using no ball, make conscientious (not just playing around) practice strokes that travel across the hole. Pay attention to see whether the putterhead crosses the center of the hole versus making an angled stroke. If the stroke is not straight across the cup with some toe or heel leading or lagging, then correct the subsequent strokes. Practice until the straight-across concept is the norm. You might have noticed professional golfers checking their putting stroke after having missed what they thought was a makeable putt. These are golfers who have years and years of dedicated practice to reach the elite level, and they still need to check their putting strokes for squareness.

Square the Putterface Drill. An extension of the previous drill offered by Glenn Deck (*Golf Magazine*, July 2010). Line up a straight

5-foot putt. Lay your putter along the target line with the end of the grip touching the ball and the putterhead closer to the hole. Insert two tees into the green where the grip meets the shaft to form a gate just somewhat wider than the ball. Mark the ball's location with a flat ball marker to maintain the ball-to-hole target line for repeated putts. Putt the ball through the gate (which should be about 12 inches in front of the ball) into the hole. If the ball touches the right tee, the putt has been pushed; if it hits the left tee, the putt has been pulled (assuming a right-handed putter). Practice until you can putt without hitting either tee. As you improve narrow the gate to force yourself to maintain a square putterface.

Consistently Missed Putts

There are two obvious consistent misses. It's difficult to state which one occurs most often because of their overlap. The two misses are leaving putts short and not playing enough break. Can you see each of these as consistent themes in your putting? If not, may I suggest you and I change places. You do the writing and I'll gladly step into your putting shoes.

Let's consider the litany of explanations why we leave putts short of the cup and are then reminded ad nauseam of some of the most well-worn cliches heard in golf: "Never up, never in"; "Putts left short seldom go in." Oh, really? I suppose the overarching reason we leave most putts short is our fear of the outcome. We don't trust our read, which leads to an inevitable drop in our putting confidence. What's the result? We run scared, our muscles tighten up, tempo and fluidity of movement is lost, and we putt defensively. Our thoughts are not on making a good stroke but rather on hoping (maybe even on desperately "praying") that we can get the putt close enough to make the next one. And, with this attitude, the next one is most certainly a reality! These pessimistic thoughts create anxiety, which keeps our uncertainty alive and fosters tight, restricted movements. Feel and touch are essential determinants of putting success, but over accentuating the intended line, for example, in favor of a multifaceted approach tends to create a problem called "line lock." This occurs most often on short putts and leaves us exasperated. Is there anything much worse and more inexcusable that leaving a putt dead on line millimeters short of the hole?

Throughout the book there are numerous mentions of the potential disruption that "noise" has on our putting plans. Remember, though, that "noise" isn't noise until you allow it to be a distraction. Here's a good example. Your playing partner "scares" you by striking his first putt way past the hole. Now, what happens to your nicely thought out plan? Have you ever uttered or heard anyone else exclaim: "Your putt scared the crap out of me"? What are the odds now that you'll leave your putt short? My suggestion is that you stay with your original read (meaning direction and distance) and consider what, if any, adjustment may be needed in the force necessary to stroke your putt. Realize what your tendency will be, and trust your adjusted plan of action. Noise created by playing partners' positioning, movements, or talking needs to serve as a signal to step back and redo your preparation so that it doesn't interfere with your putt. In fact, if you are tightly focused on your putting routine, you might even make yourself immune to potential distractions.

Golfers often find it necessary (a putting confidence ploy) to comment about the outcome of their putts. "Wow, that putt wasn't even close"; "What kept that putt out?"; "Nobody could have come close to making that putt!"; and so on . . . and on. Sometimes our minds cause us to think in weird ways but maybe none as neurotic as Joe Parent suggests in *Zen Putting*. He proposes that there is more saving face in leaving a putt short than long because of the positive comments you can make. "I had it, all I needed to do was hit it"; "I had it read perfectly"; and "Just to get that putt close was a major accomplishment." This *subtle mental manipulate*, as Parent terms it, serves the purpose of salvaging something positive out of a negative outcome. But, perhaps if our minds are this devious, this is the reason we miss putts. This is something you'll have to judge for yourself. I've already made my "clinical diagnosis."

You may recall the earlier point, really an admonition, that golfers ought to double the amount of break they see on breaking putts. Choosing an aimline low of the hole has absolutely no chance of success, whereas a high aimline gives you hope. Play around with this

2x concept on the practice green and assess its effectiveness, but do it in concert with determining the fall line.

Sometimes consistent misses are caused by a lack of awareness or, in other words, being blind to the obvious. Any golfer who doesn't realize that almost every putt misses on the low side, that putts stopping short of the hole never go in, and that putts struck off line always leave a next putt is doomed. If the person really doesn't care about performance or score, so be it. But, most golfers I know don't fall into this category. As any behavior analyst will tell you, awareness is the first step to change. In the case that self-awareness is lacking, outside assistance is called for. If you have a playing partner who doesn't recognize his or her consistent putting shortcomings, as a friend you need to gently point these out and offer some advice if you're capable. And, remember, your friendly golf professional is always there to assist you.

Consistent misses also result from a lack of adjustment to the conditions. How many times have you heard yourself or your playing partners complain that you couldn't get the ball to the hole all day or conversely that you struck every putt long? If the greens are fast or slow, make that assessment early in the round, and visualize your end target either long or short of the hole. Or, move a few steps closer to the hole on fast greens and practice the stroke needed for the shorter length putt, then move back and putt with the stroke previously practiced. On slow greens, just do the reverse. Take a few steps back from the ball, make the necessary practice strokes, step up to the ball and putt. As we're constantly reminded, doing the same thing over and over and expecting different results is insanity. And, sure, the game drives us crazy but why increase the craziness by a simple failure to adapt.

> For leaving putts short: Plan to stroke the ball 10-17 inches beyond the hole.

> For leaving putts low of the hole: Double the amount of break and start the ball on this aimline.

For directional issues: Line the ball's logo along the intended aimline and putt as if the putt's a straight putt.

For control of your putting, including mental control: Be systematic, regimented, and unchanging in your pre-putt preparation and putting routine

The last reason for consistently missing putts might be classified as mechanical. Being last in this list doesn't at all indicate it's the least important. Consistent errors in alignment, grip, head position, and several others beget consistent misses. On the other hand, looking up too soon is not a mechanical error because it's a direct function of the image-of-achievement. In fact, looking up to see the outcome is more neuropsychological than anything. Scott Peck refers to this as the *paradox of eagerness*. This is such an apt descriptor because it captures the essence of another of golf's great adages: "If you look up to see a good shot, you'll never see it." When you're so concerned with the outcome that you just can't wait to see what happens, your impatience and lack of discipline will be your undoing. And, what does it say about your trust factor when you don't exercise the discipline to complete the stroke before you need to peek? I hope you can see that being outcome-oriented rather than focusing on your putting stroke is dangerous. If you tend to have this problem, then consciously loading in positive reminders such as "See the putterface strike the ball"; "See the ball travel over a pre-selected mark an inch in front of the ball"; or "Wait until the putterhead passes the original ball position" might be useful. The real key is building the discipline to practice staying down at least until the ball leaves the putterface.

If you find that you are making good reads and believe you're stroking the putts well but the ball continually burns the edges, then it's time to check your ball contact. Are you really making square contact with the ball? You can check this with the following drill.

Stay On-Line Drill. From *Golf Magazine*, May 2009. Collect a few range balls (hopefully not out of your golf bag, although I knew someone who put identifying marks on range balls and thought it was mighty nice of the club to furnish golf balls to play with—a true story) and draw a line around each ball, using a gadget like Line M Up found in many pro shops. On the practice green locate a straight 8- to 10-foot putt. Line a ball up to the hole and putt. Putt a few more. Watch the line on the ball. Does it roll straight or does it wobble? Any wobble means that the putt was not struck squarely. Practice until the line on the putted ball stays on the target line.

Good and Bad Putting Days

I remind you again that all human behavior is normally distributed. There will be good putting days and bad putting days for all golfers—duffers and major champions alike. It's not uncommon even for the best golfers in the world to shoot 63 one day and post 71 the next day. At all levels of golf ability, scores are ruled by putting. The point to recognize, however, is that you need not increase the incidence of bad putting days by faulty thought processes. Don't allow your thoughts and emotions to be your downfall. They can be your strengths or your weaknesses, you get to choose which. Don't discount the fact that some mechanical glitches might have popped into your putting. One of my old tournament partners used to claim that when putts consistently lip out or run the edges, you're likely moving your head during the stroke. Possible. Also, ball position may have been altered unconsciously, or perhaps there are issues with stance, putter take away, etc. These factors and their corrections other than those already discussed I leave to those more qualified to deal with the mechanics of putting.

As you ride the wave of success on your good putting days, everything flows, and it seems you can do no wrong. You see the read clearly, you putt confidently, and everything seems to fall in. It's almost as if you're on automatic pilot. Your partners rave about the day you're having: "You're putting out of your mind," they exclaim. Have you had a day like this? If so, congratulations! If not, have you looked on while others had these highlight reels? If I may be allowed to interject a personal note, I can remember playing so well on a particular day that I just "had" to play a second 18 holes. However, I found it difficult to explain this "absolute need" to the "keeper of the gate" when I arrived home late, if you know what I mean.

Success is sometimes the putting devil in disguise because good putting days are temporary, and unfortunately we know what's coming. Why doesn't our putting success last? After all, we must have the talent to perform at high levels because yesterday's score card shows it. Let's explore some possibilities. One reason stares us in the face. We tend to play to our handicaps (measures of our usual talent), meaning that our scores are distributed around our average. There are outliers on each end of our putting continuums, yet following a great putting day, we can normally expect that the next day's performance will regress toward our average. It's this way for all golfers, even those professionals who are multimillionaires. A second reason is that success doesn't teach us much, if anything, because we're so caught up in the warm and fuzzy feeling of "doing good." Who in their right mind wants to ask "why" when things are going so well? That's going to interrupt the flow. I understand this, but failure to contemplate the reasons for the atypical success at some later point in time is going to end up being a problem (or a solution missed). Why? Because we'll never know what caused us to putt so well and, therefore, we'll never know how to recreate the super-competent image-of-achievement. As I keep reminding you, putting is indeed brain science, and you know what is required to create a successful plan of action. If the logic escapes you, then may I suggest you go back and scan the chapter dealing with this explanation. The last reason rather piggybacks on the previous reason. When we "putt out of our minds" or nonconsciously, we tend to lose, forget, or fail to attend consciously to one or more significant perceptual cues that will eventually unhinge our performance. This temporary "flight of fancy" leads us to false performance evaluation. I heard David Duval being interviewed some time ago. You may recall that David was World #1 in 1999, and he has fought more than a decade-long uphill battle to return to any semblance of his former playing self. He spoke of losing his way because he gradually slipped away from the fundamentals that got him to the top. What did he lose? The perceptual and conceptual cues that produce competent golf swings and putts. Putting with confidence is good but competent plans must be in the picture or a crash is imminent. Having a sense that you're bulletproof is nice but eventually one bullet will seek you out. Reality hurts!

Did you ever get on the "bogey train" and couldn't find your way off for several holes, or maybe even for the whole round? Of course you have. It's contagious, isn't it? I wonder if you might be punching your train ticket for a longer trip than is necessary? To continue this analogy, you are the engineer of your putting stroke and the way you think and feel about it. If you miss parring the easiest hole on the course by an unfortunate 3-putt, what's your response? Do you <u>forgive-forget</u>? Or do you harbor the abhorrent distaste for the next few holes? Remember that your plan of action, the image-of-achievement, incorporates past experiences into the next putt. One bad putt can lead to the next bad putt if you don't break the cycle. A missed putt adds an additional stroke to your score, thereby putting extra pressure on your next putt to keep things under control or to get that stroke back. This is faulty thinking—this isn't tennis! Once the stroke is made it goes down on the scorecard never to be erased, that is unless you have a creative scorekeeper with an eraser on his pencil. By now, you most likely know what I'm going to suggest you do. Go through your entire routine (green reading, pre-putt preparation, and ritual), giving full attention to the putt. This eliminates the opportunity for your loose-lip mind to shout out things like "What's the use, the round is over for me"; "I've just gotta make this putt"; "This is my last chance, miss it and you might as well go home." Hopefully you say that none of this makes any sense to you because you never hear such self-talk. If I thought I could believe you, I'd be happy for you but . . . .

Some days more than others you have to accept the reality of the game. Holes are cut in difficult locations on the greens, your iron shots aren't as close as usual, you're consistently putting over ridges, etc. Sometimes reading greens is difficult, even to the point that all the professional golfers misread a particular putt on a given day. These conditions are likely adding strokes to most golfers' scores, not just to your score. Failure to accept reality, especially when there's no likelihood of changing the situation, is grounds for an exceedingly aggravating round of golf. So, keep things in perspective, control thoughts and emotions, and let one missed putt count only one stroke and not create a cumulative effect by increasing the likelihood of missing future putts.

What Do You Trust?

Recall the earlier scenarios: You aim your putt outside left of the cup because this particular putt "always" breaks left to right, but you MISS. You aim your ball inside left and plan to stroke the putt firmly to take out the break but the ball still breaks off the right edge, and you MISS. Your playing partner's ball breaks left at the hole; your putt from a similar spot fails to break, and you MISS. So, what do you trust—your read, your memory, a recent experience? Not an easy answer, is it? I've played on greens that create optical illusions—uphill is really downhill and downhill is really uphill. On other greens, apparent subtle breaks are really huge breaks. The answer has to be couched in "if . . . then" terms. If you're a very good reader of greens and you understand the reality of breaking putts, then go with your read. If you're not a good green reader or if you have doubts about a particular putt, then go with what you glean from previous putts. But, be careful to assess not just the outcome of another's putt but also the particular characteristics of the golfer. For instance, does he cut the ball and impart spin? Is she a bold or tentative putter? Is his stroke rhythmical or does he pop the ball on contact? Take particular notice of the length of the backstroke and forward stroke. Watch intently if you want to pick up cues that might help you.

But, what if it comes down to an inner conflict? Do you trust your read of the putt or do trust your memory from past similar putts? The current putt looks dead straight (although 95% of putts have some break), but your experience tells you that all putts on this hole break to the water, or to the mountains, or to the back of the green—whatever. I agonize over this dilemma because it's one I face continually. And I believe that most other golfers do likewise even though they might not verbalize it. It would be folly to completely disregard past outcomes as this dismisses the importance of experience. Golfers perform better if and when they learn from their putting experiences. On the other hand, those golfers who are good putters are successful to a large part because they are good at reading greens. Although I might not be the last word on this issue, here's my suggested resolution. Initially go through your normal green reading routine, choosing an aimline and corresponding feel or touch needed to have the putt travel its planned path into the cup. But, then adjust the aimline to the amount that your experience suggests the ball might break. Instead of planning on the putt going straight, hedge your bet by playing the ball to the apparent high side but not so much that the putt would miss if indeed it doesn't break.

Excessive Three Putting

I know what you're saying, even one 3-putt is one too many, and I would agree. But reality must carry the day. You will 3-putt and the most proficient putters in the world will 3-putt. The issue here is multiple 3-putts in a round that totally destroy any hopes for a good score. The cause of most 3-putts is obvious: your iron shots to the greens or chips from the fringe leave you too far from the hole. Dave Pelz's research shows than golfers with handicaps in the 20-30 range tend to 3-putt around 20% of the time, that's 3-4 times a round. Eliminating 3-putts altogether (we're being very optimistic here) would reduce these golfers score by 3-4 strokes. Consider what this would mean to your score, handicap, and attitude.

Perhaps you don't have a putting problem. Maybe you're simply a bad iron player or a poor chipper. Facetiously, I would urge you to hit your irons closer to the pins and chip better. Maybe just hit your chips closer because you might be missing a lot of greens. But seriously, practicing to become a better chipper will really reduce your 3-putts. But, that's another story and we want to address the issue of poor putting. The most likely culprit leading to 3-putts is leaving your first putt too far away from the hole, likely too short. You need to become a better lag putter but, rather than trying to putt the ball within the proverbial 3-foot circle, I'd suggest you try to make every putt you attempt. Why give up the chance of making it? Saying "Just get it close" is akin to the professional golfer saying "I just need par on the last hole to win the tournament," or you saying "I just need a par on the last hole to shoot my best score ever." Do you see the inherent negativity in this kind of self-talk? Do you assume that it's easier to lag the ball close to the hole by just trying to get it close or by trying to make it? And, furthermore, what kind of plan of action does your brain create with "just get it close"? It seems to me that planning to make every putt is the preferred approach. And to the issue of making the second putt, which would you find easier: putting a ball that never reached the hole so you have no idea how it breaks at the end, or putting a ball that you saw roll long of the hole with a now known visible break? Doesn't seem like a difficult choice! If your experience corresponds with mine, I make more putts coming back to the hole than when I leave the first putt short. There's two very good reasons for this, and I'm not certain which is more important but I have my druthers. I bet my attitude is typical of most golfers when I leave a putt woefully short—I'm a little disgusted with my attempt. This doesn't leave me in the best frame of mind to attempt the second putt, that is until I gather my emotions and control my typical self-labeling. I'm not going to disclose any of my favorite comments but let me say they're a little stronger than "Oh, my" (channeling Annie in the movie *Bull Durham*). It probably would take you no more than a nanosecond to conjure up your favorite labels. If you don't or won't give up your negative thoughts and emotions, then it's difficult to the give the second putt the singular focus needed to make a positive stroke. Negativity creates "noise" in the system. On the other hand, when I stroke the first putt beyond the hole, I'm not happy but I don't have the same negative feeling because I feel I gave the putt an opportunity to go in. Plus I have some additional sensory information to make a more accurate plan of action for my second attempt.

Even if you happen to stroke the first putt close to the hole, there's still the issue of closing the deal. Nothing is more deflating than missing a 3-4 foot second putt after getting the 30-40 foot putt that close to the hole. There's a real expectation that you should make the short putt because, after all, the hard part of getting it close from all that distance is over. Be careful. Give the short putt its due because it can be missed. You might want to return to the section above dealing with missed short putts to shore up your thinking.

Putting Yips

I hope you can skip this section because you don't even recognize the problem. But, unfortunately, some of our golfing fraternity/sorority suffer this malady. If you watched Hank Haney try to help Charles Barkley over several sessions televised on the Golf Channel, you get a good picture of what the yips look like. Apply this picture to putting and you'll get the picture of a disconnected herky-jerky stroke, almost to the point where the putter can't even be taken back to make a stroke. The condition doesn't impact long putts, only short ones. Putters who have the yips know they're likely going to miss, and the TV audience cringes at the likelihood of seeing a professional golfer miss a putt that is almost automatic for the rest of the field. And, just so you appreciate that yips are not just the purview of less talented golfers, perhaps you'll recognize some of the following names who unfortunately toiled under the dark clouds of the yips—Arnold Palmer, Johnny Miller, Craig Stadler, and Beth Daniel. This not an exhaustive list but illustrates the point that not even the best golfers in the world are immune.

Clearly there are mechanical deficiencies (e.g., quick tempo, jerky backstroke, overacceleration, tight grip, moving head, and perhaps others) that predispose putting failures. What do you suppose is the factor responsible for all these errors? Surely you understand that thoughts predispose actions, and the nature of actions described above must have been derived from faulty thinking. Basically, yips are primarily mental; more specifically they're caused by a loss of confidence and loss of control. Loss of what, you might ask? Loss of the process that creates the product. Look carefully at the litany of putting errors described below, and put yourself in the shoes of a golfer who experiences the following before he putts:

* sees and feels the putt miss before he putts

* is fully aware of how bad the situation is

* hears negative self-talk ("Don't miss another one")

* understands the putt should be made ("Anybody could sink this one")

* realizes how foolish he'll look if he can't make an "easy" short putt

* has a certain degree of self-loathing about her incompetent putting

If you had the yips, you would be shocked if you didn't exhibit some of the same aforementioned behaviors, wouldn't you? I know I would. As any golfer goes through his pre-putt routine, would you recommend any of the above thoughts or feelings? Of course not. Can you picture trying to focus on choosing your aimline in concert with the feel necessary to make the successful stroke with all this mumbo-jumbo going on inside your head? Return to the image of Charles Barkley's golf swing, if you can, and you have what's commonly called "paralysis by analysis." There's information overload because so much is going on simultaneously that it's no wonder those who suffer from putting yips can barely initiate a swing or stroke. And, if it is initiated, it's uncoordinated, out of phase, poorly timed—call it what you will—but the end result will not be good.

Some golfers never recover from the putting yips, and it spells doom to their playing days. I suggest we look to the problem to attempt to create a solution. I claimed earlier that yips are a result of lack of control and loss of confidence. Several writers have addressed this problem and offered solutions but often the proposals have been isolated and not bound by any systematic framework. Let's start with control because if you can't control your thoughts and feelings you have no chance of resurrecting your putting. Controlling thoughts is not easy because you will continually run internal dialog until your life expires. And sometimes thoughts will be irrational, downright dangerous, and will act as saboteurs. Thoughts run rampant but they have a sequential nature. One thought occurs, degrades, and another takes its place. It is impossible to eliminate the thought process and go "brain dead," so to speak. Here's a test for you: STOP. Think no thoughts for the next 5 seconds. You couldn't do this for even a fraction of a second. Try it again. Are we doomed to be a slave to our thoughts and allow ourselves to be led down paths we don't want to travel? Fortunately, we can exert some control. If you're facing the yips, you must develop a very deliberate, step-by-step pre-putt routine that never varies one iota from one putt to the next. Total attention to a systematic plan takes up mental space and reduces the chance of a random and irrational thought from creeping in. The next time you're watching golf on TV pay attention to the consistency of the golfers' routines and rituals, especially how they step into the ball, look down their aimlines, then look back to the ball before they putt. I like the suggestion of

Cohn and Winters to track your target with your eyes up and down the target line (not by moving your head just your eyes), perhaps two or three times, and then make the stroke when your eyes return to the ball on the final cycle. The image of your target or ball path will decay in less than 2 seconds, so standing over the ball for more than this time frame is contraindicated. If you can fill time with your planned agenda, then you can begin to take control of the mental environment.

Even though I've addressed the issues of gaining control and feeling confident separately, they are integrated items—one without the other is like Sonny without Cher or like Brooks without Dunn. The first step in gaining confidence is believing you can conquer the yips, or at least minimize their impact. It's not the stroke that's the <u>primary</u> cause of the problem, it's the outcome. Therefore, it might be a good idea to putt to a tee or to a round cardboard coaster (get a friend to pick one up at a local tavern). This will free you up to focus on the stroke without worrying about making the putt, while at the same time offering you a target. Teach yourself to visualize the aimline and the target. The closer your problem is to the terminal stage of "yippyness," the more practice you need. Thousands of trials are essential to retrain your mind and your stroke. Once you feel a reasonable level of confidence, stroke short putts into the cup over and over, making sure to use your routine. One way to overcome the apparent need to forego your routine is to use a circle drill around the hole so each putt is different. Once you reach a comfort level move the distance back and keep repeating the process. In your practice sessions, be really aware of the immediate feeling leading to a yipped putt and stop, step back, redo the preparation, and putt. Recognize what it feels like so you can consciously intercede and prevent the poor putt from occurring. Eventually it will come time to test your competence by putting under pressure—self-induced or putting against another golfer. Don't be surprised if you experience peaks and valleys during your practice phase because that's natural. Don't get upset with relapses, they'll happen, just go back to the fundamentals and start again. With every trial executed properly you are retraining your putting stroke and developing neurological competence.

Some golfers with the yips go so far as to change their putting grip (e.g., left hand low, claw) or even change their putters (usually from a regular length putter to a long putter), This drastic change creates a feeling of starting over by leaving the ill-working putting style in the past. This may be just temporary but might even become permanent. The point is to change the stroke from uncoordinated to one with tempo. Before we leave our discussion of the yips, I would like to point out the work of Marius Filmalter (see mariusgolf.com) on this problem. He addressed the issue of loss of control (*Golf Magazine*, January 2013; *Golf Magazine*, April 2013) but more in the physical domain, but he too attributes this loss to mental stress. To remediate the jerkiness that tends to increase toward the end of the stroke, he recommends adopting the old-time "pop" stroke, currently utilized by the current putting wizard, Brandt Snedeker. Basically, pop the ball but restrict the follow-through, thereby reducing the flailing or oscillating putterhead. Most golfers control their putting stroke with the palm of their trailing hand. So, that's where the loss of putterhead control originates. To minimize this control, Filmalter advocates a claw-type grip but with the palm of the trailing hand on top of the grip, facing one's chest and not facing the target. Why? To reduce the dominance of the hand that's creating the problem. Play around with each of these suggestions and assess their effectiveness for you.

But, one again, I must repeat the inevitable—change will take hard work and lots of deliberate practice. Don't even think you can make any improvement with a little bit of casual practice here and there. Find something you like, something that works for you, and commit to some serious practice sessions.

Failure to Transfer Putting Practice to the Course

I don't suppose you've ever expressed surprise, maybe even aggravation, that your successes on the driving range or putting green failed to match your subsequent performance on the course, have you? We all get into zany thinking modes about the expected positive relationship between practice performance and game performance. Allow me to add an exception to the above assertion because I believe most really proficient golfers play as they practice. If you've ever heard a football or basketball coach being interviewed, you've undoubtedly heard the above principle expressed: "We tend to play as we practice." Back to zany thinking. I wonder if anyone has sometimes shared the practice-performance relationship I've experienced at times? If I've hit shots badly on the range or made very few practice putts before the round, then this signals I'll have a good day? Perhaps there are golfers out there who think just the opposite. If their pre-round practice is good, then this is bound to lead to poor on-course performance. This really doesn't make a lot of sense, does it? Since I raised the issue of nonsense thinking, let me offer you another example. Many years ago, when I first started playing golf, there was a low single digit handicap golfer at my course who wouldn't allow himself to make a par on the first hole. When his second shot reached the par 4 hole in two, he'd try to make the birdie but failing this, he would putt twice more to make a bogey. Why? Because he was convinced that if he parred the first hole, it would lead to a poor round. This example is a little removed from the practice-performance issue but it's in the same vein, that one's previous performance should predict a later one.

Let's take a more in-depth analysis at the discrepancy between practice and performance. First, we're incorrect in labeling what we do before we play as practice. It's not practice, far from it—it's a kind of a warm-up. Do you think the way a basketball team performs the traditional pre-game two-line lay-up drill is a real causative factor in determining their upcoming performance? Probably not! They do it to warm-up, get acclimated, maybe get motivated, whatever. Now, of course, if you make an unusual number of putts on the practice green, then your putting confidence will receive a boost and might lead to good on-course putting, but not necessarily. Ask yourself whether the demands of putting on a practice green before your round are anywhere close to the demands of putting during your round. How many differences can you list? Here are some questions to prime your thinking.

> Are the characteristics of the greens on the course the same as on the practice green?

> Are your thoughts and emotions following your missed putts on the practice green the same as on the course?

Are putts on the practice green as important as putts on the course?

Do you get "do-overs" on the course like you do on the practice green?

Are the time constraints similar for on-course and practice green putting?

Have you come to any conclusions about why there's a discrepancy between pre-round putting and on-course putting? It seems to come down to one obvious fact. Because the two tasks only have the mechanics of stroking putts in common, why should we expect there to be much, if any, transfer. If we are expecting any performance transfer from the practice green to actual on-course performance, then we need to deliberately practice under the conditions we'll experience on the course. Then, and only then, should we expect to see transfer. When professional golfers get ready for their rounds, they realistically expect some parallels between their pre-round rehearsals because of the degree to which their skills are ingrained. Warm-up for them is just a test of how things are working on a given day. But, even at their level of expertise, there's probably little that happens on the range or putting green that leads them to believe a score of 63 is in the offing. Having said this, there is certainly one very important aspect that we should expect to transfer from the practice green to the course: namely, the speed of the greens on a given day. Green speed will determine the length of backstroke needed for specific distances (refer to previous drills to gauge distances) as well as the amount of break expected on various type putts. Repetition is the key to learning, so I'll repeat myself here. Transfer of putting performance from practice to game will only occur if your practice (even though it might be short because the starter has called you to the tee) is planned to discover the condition of the greens. It really doesn't take long to check the distance-speed feel of a number of putts. Nor does it take long to finish your practice with a number successfully made 3-footers. From the numerous drills laid out earlier, pick out two or three and use them routinely before you play.

SEVEN. QUEST FOR COMPETENCE AND CONFIDENCE

I just tell myself I'm the best putter on the planet. Vijay Singh

I guess deep inside, I'm twenty years old and feel I can make every putt I look at. Tiger Woods, early in his professional career

Do you approach your putts with the attitude that Vijay and Tiger espoused above? What a foolish question to ask, right? You're not in their class so how could you expect to have their extreme positive expectations? And, yet, haven't you had some days when nobody in the world could have putted any better than you? What about the day you strung three or four consecutive birdies together? Could ANYONE have beaten you? And what about those long, double breaking putts that miraculously fell in the hole? Wouldn't you put this performance up against anyone in the world? What I'm suggesting is that we all have been there, just not as often and consistently as we would like. Putting success just like success in all other achievement-oriented endeavors is determined primarily by your level of confidence. At this point your cynical side might say that it's easy for golfers like Vijay and Tiger to be confident because of how successful they've been and how successful they're likely to be in the future: "When I start putting like Tiger, look out, I'll feel like I can make everything I look at." To this brash assertion I think your golfing buddies would almost quizzically reply: "How long will we have to wait to see this?" You reply: "Well . . . well . . . just you wait." Basically, you have no answer to the question "when" or "how." You've fallen into the typical human belief that putting confidence is a <u>consequence</u> of putting success, and in an obvious way you're not entirely wrong—but really only partially correct.

But, have you ever considered that putting confidence needs to <u>precede</u> any chance for consistent success? This is rather like the chicken-and-egg dilemma—which comes first? Good putters make more putts than poor putters, so for good putters putting confidence is a natural outcome. It's easy to feel confidently when your putts are falling. On the other hand, unless a certain degree of confidence exists in the planning stages before the putt is stroked, even good putters reduce their chances for success because they'll putt defensively. There are good arguments on both sides, leaving one rather perplexed. However, regarding the relationship of putting confidence and putting success, I want to offer you my perspective that you need a certain degree of putting confidence or you'll have little chance of being successful. To this end you need to know something about putting confidence, its various components, how it can increase your positive outlook on putting, and strategies and drills to enhance it.

In a previous chapter we explored, albeit briefly, how the brain works to create plans of action called images-of-achievement. In essence, there will <u>always</u> be an outcome to any plan (e.g., stroke a 10-foot right-to-left breaking putt—you either made or missed it), but it <u>will not always</u> be the outcome you desire. Remember, though, it really will be the outcome you planned (or failed to plan—it makes no difference to your brain) because you were in charge of inputting the data. To the degree you miss something important (e.g., degree of downhill slope) or add something (e.g., a negative image or thought), your incorrect planning will create a flawed image-of-achievement. What do you think you can expect from this self-created neurological incompetence? The answer is simple, isn't it: a putt that has no chance of going in the hole.

The chart below serves to indicate the development of competent putting performance, how competence impacts on putting confidence, and the four essential building blocks of putting confidence. Direct your attention to the two-way or double-directional arrows that indicate both cause and effect. Spend a little time looking at the chart.

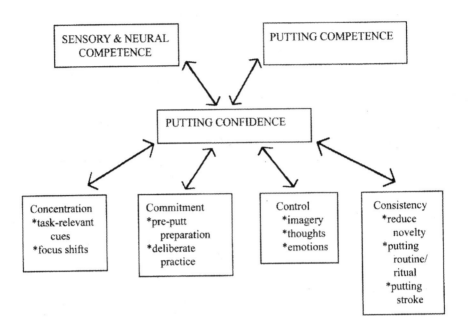

Putting Competence/Putting Confidence Interactional Model

In your pre-putt preparation process of selecting all the task-relevant cues from the irrelevant cues, and assuming your decisions are correct, you provide your brain with accurate data. And when your brain receives the perceptual data and then adds conceptual information based on past experiences (e.g., feel for the distance), an image-of-achievement is readied to be put into action. Assuming you don't sabotage the plan by adding an unexpected distraction (e.g., "I hope I can come close"), you have achieved sensory and neural competence for the upcoming putt. To the degree that your plan of action is correct, you will have a successful putt. This doesn't necessarily mean that the putt will be made, only that you did everything you could to execute the best stroke. But, as you've read earlier, not all well-struck putts fall in.

Back to the arrows in the chart that point both ways. It means that there is a reciprocal or two-way relationship between terms, meaning basically that there is an interactional cause and effect relationship occurring simultaneously. Look at the top line of the chart. The more competence you develop as a putter, the sharper will be your green reading skills because you won't be distracted by woeful thoughts, and the more positive will be your memory traces because the input will be on target. And, the more sensory and neural competence you develop, the better you'll putt because your plan of action will be clear. So, basically, as one improves, so does the other. But, I must cautiously add, as one malfunctions, so does the other. Can you stop here and create for yourself the damaging downside scenario? I hope I've been able to explain this so-called "reciprocal determinism" because this concept runs through the entire chart.

Putting Confidence

The degree of putting competence you demonstrate round after round, based on your putting successes, will directly influence how positively you feel about your putting (i.e., how much putting confidence you have). Would you say you're an excellent putter? a good putter? a fair putter? a disaster? This attitude or feeling is going to affect both sensory and conceptual competence and impact putting competence. I hope you can grasp that a high level of confidence enhances how a golfer will read greens and what kinds of memories will tend to unfold. If this is not clear, suffice it to say that golfers who putt poorly are not likely going to spend a great deal of time preparing for a task that provides little benefit or enjoyment. Additionally low putting confidence tends to undermine one's putting competence by a whole bunch of factors (e.g., negative feeling and emotions, self-deprecation, and a host of others that will be discussed in more detail later in the chapter).

Is there anyone in the world who fails to comprehend what self-confidence means to performance, not from a definitional perspective but from experience? Certainly high achievers understand it better than others because they realize how significant it is to their success. Consider two highly skilled golfers (choose any two). They're very close in their skill level—there's very little variance—and they both have won major tournaments. But, on any given day, their attitude or more correctly their psychological frame of mind might be worlds apart. Skill is relatively stable; psyches fluctuate. By the time you're finished reading this chapter and have digested its contents, if I've done my job to explain things adequately, I believe you'll agree with me that self-confidence is really the key to successful performance and to anything else you'll pursue in life.

Let me offer you a brief glimpse into how some well recognized professional golfers view confidence.

> *It takes years to build up your confidence, but it hardly takes a moment to lose it. Confidence is when you stand over a shot and you know you're going to make it because you've done it time and time again.* Jack Nicklaus

> *It'll be a slow progression as far as I'm not trying to go from not very good right now to perfect . . . . The idea is to take one step at a time and build up some confidence.* Jim Furyk, May 2009.

> *When you've been where I've been, you have no confidence in putting . . . . I was coasting everything up to the hole and wasn't giving the hole a scare. In March 1 looked like an absolute fool.* Ernie Els, *told to Golfweek*, July 27, 2012

> *Confidence is something you need to protect at all costs . . . . confidence just goes away. It's a slow thing. So it's slow putting (it) back together.* David Duval, told to *Golfweek*, July 11, 2012

> *I'm not crazy about being on the putting green. I don't like practicing it. I don't like it in tournaments. That's probably 50 percent of my problem with it. So I need to assess my attitude towards putting, and I think that would probably go a long way into helping me putt better.* Jason Dufner, told to *Golfweek*, June 1, 2012

The bedrock is total self-belief. Rory McIlroy, told to *Golfweek*, September 14, 2012.

What can we learn from the above statements? I see several important points:

* Confidence takes a long time to acquire.

* Confidence is not stable, it can be lost in a moment—or does it degrade slowly?

* Confidence has to be built gradually in sequential steps.

* Confidence doesn't indicate perfection.

* Confidence isn't something you can touch or see, it's a feeling or attitude that you can perform a particular task.

* Confidence is based on the attitude you have about the task.

* Confidence will determine how hard you work at a task.

* Confidence is a trait all talented golfers recognize and protect.

* Confidence is absolutely essential to achieve high level performance.

Perhaps you can think of a time when you were extremely confident about some aspect of your life. And, hopefully, you've had enough great putting days to know what putting confidence feels like. It's almost assured that you've had putting days at the other end of the spectrum so you know the difference. Do you feel differently about your ability to perform the various demands golf places on you—driving, iron play, bunker play, chipping, and putting? Do you find that confidence in one aspect of your game carries over into another part? Do you know any golfers who are good drivers of the golf ball but are just fair or poor putters? Or does your experience tell you that golfers who are good at one aspect of the game are equally adept at other aspects? The point I'm getting is that, like competence, our confidence is task-specific. In fact, look back at the chart and you'll see the reciprocal relationship between competence and confidence. It isn't difficult to understand that good driving (high competence) leads to positive thoughts and feelings (high confidence) about tee shots, whereas poor putting (low competence) leads to negative thoughts and feelings (low confidence) on the greens.

Which of the following professional golfers do you suppose had the better career putting statistics? Dave Stockton, who claimed he never saw a putt he didn't think he could make? Or Ben Hogan, who almost wished putting would be "legislated" out of the game and that ball striking should be elevated to the most important aspect of golf? If you answered, Dave Stockton, then give yourself some applause. At the time Jason Dufner made the aforementioned statements, he was ranked 103 (strokes gained) on the PGA Tour. Do you think attitude matters?

Some more "experienced" golfers might be asking: "What's the big deal with putting confidence? Just step up and make the putt." If that works for you, who am I to judge, but I hope for your sake that you're not trying to fool yourself. I sincerely believe that you cannot be a consistently good putter without being confident. That's all the more important because there are many trials that golfers will undoubtedly face that tend to try their patience and impinge on their positive attitude. Consider just a couple of examples. Your golf group travels to an away course where you find the greens are very sloped and undulating. On such greens, by the end of the round it will likely be easy for you to conclude that you're a bad putter. That is unless you can accept the fact that nobody in your group putted these greens well. If you can't convince yourself that these greens were not a true test of your putting ability or that you just weren't yourself today (i.e., you suspend reality), you're putting confidence will suffer.

What would be the true test of a golfer's confidence? Standing over a putt to win a two-dollar Nassau, a match, a club championship, or the Masters? Positive feelings wane as the golfer's heart beats faster, breathing is strained, muscles tense, thoughts run rampant, and motivation to make the putt creates a "make-it-or-die" experience. Yet, consider Sergio Garcia's and Vijay Singh's putting accomplishments under championship pressure. On the first extra hole of the 2008 PGA

Championship, both golfers made 20-foot birdie putts back-to-back to prolong the tournament. This was a WOW moment if you saw it. Each golfer believed, they prepared perfectly, and their strokes matched their intent. Could we have made that 20-foot putt under those conditions, or would we have folded like the proverbial cheap suit?

A logical question golfers might legitimately ask at this point might be: "My golfing experiences have showed me repeatedly how important putting confidence is to my mental well-being on the golf course, but how can I get more of it?" Some answers will come from practicing some of the confidence putting drills that follow immediately, and more will be derived from an elaboration of the four major building blocks shown on the chart, namely concentration, commitment, control, and consistency.

Putting Confidence Drills

What are the task demands of putting?

* Developing a sense of being able to read the correct line

* Developing a sense of stroking the putt the correct distance

* Developing a sense that you can make putts consistently

* Developing a feeling that you can make putts in pressure situations

* Developing the ability to quickly and accurately analyze and correct errors

* Managing all the many demands that putting requires

Drills that deal with the first two demands have already been described in the mystery of reading greens chapter. The following drills are designed specifically to engender a positive feeling about your putting, you know the attitude that Jack Nicklaus referred to as standing over a putt knowing you're going to make it.

Phil's Drill. Encircle the hole with 6-8 balls 2-3 feet away and make them all or start over. Stay until you make all the balls. Repeat-repeat-repeat. This is an especially good drill just prior to playing to impart a sense of confidence in your mind.

David Frost's 4-Corner Drill. Described in an earlier chapter but repeated here. From a distance of 3 feet from the hole, putt balls at the right and left edges of the hole until you can see how far from the middle you can stroke the putt and still make it. This will give you a sense of how large the cup really is and how much room for error you have and still hole the putt. Repeat the drill with the intent to just die the putt over the front edge, and then reverse your plan to see how hard you can stroke the putt at the back edge of the cup and still have it drop. The latter will be particularly helpful in convincing you that you can stroke short putts hard enough to take out any break. Test this out by repeating the "back of the cup" concept on short breaking putts. Bang them until they jump out! Practice this enough so you won't be afraid to take the learned feelings to the course.

Dottie's Drill. On a flat green insert tees at 3-, 5-, and 7-foot distances. Place 3 balls at 3 feet and putt until you make all three. Miss one, start the sequence all over. When successful, move to 5 feet and repeat the process. Miss one, start the sequence all over at the 3-foot mark. When successful at 3- and 5 feet, then move to 7 feet and repeat the sequence. Miss any putt and return to the 3-foot distance. Bob Rotella says that sometimes Dottie Pepper, renowned LPGA golfer, would sometimes complete this drill in 10 minutes, whereas at other times it might take an hour. Got a day to spare to take this challenge? I think you can see that the idea of always having to return to the starting point will place pressure on you to concentrate and make every putt and, also, that pressure will increase the further up the success ladder you climb. Miss the last 7-foot putt when the sun is starting to go down and it will be a long night!

Don't Overthink Drill. This drill is taken from Jeff Ritter. Encircle the cup 2 feet away with 6-8 balls and move quickly around and putt all balls into the cup. Don't stop if you miss. Repeat the sequence. Short putts should be almost automatic unless you allow "noise" to disrupt the intended plan.

How Many Can You Make Drill. Encircle the cup 3 feet away with 6-8 balls. Putt the balls into the hole keeping track of how many you can make. Keep repeating the drill, moving your count upwards. Try this with a partner and see who wins within a prescribed time period.

Negative Plan/Positive Outcome Drill. This entails a game of "who do you trust?" Sometimes you have all the good intentions to make a putt but something happens at the exact moment of truth and you putt badly. This "something" is usually a disruptive negative thought (e.g., "Don't miss this putt") or a positive directive stated badly (e.g., "Stay down through the putt" meaning "Don't raise you head"). The stroke has been initiated and it's too late to stop. Does "noise" always lead to poor performance? Try this drill with some 3- to 4-foot putts. Read them, develop a good plan of action, step into the putt, but just before pulling the trigger say to yourself (or aloud if no one is within earshot) "I can't make this putt." Try it with some of your personal favorite admonitions (e.g., "Don't raise your head"; Don't pull it"; Don't push it"; "Don't hit it too hard"; "Don't whiff it"). The essence of the drill appears to speak against everything I described earlier in the chapter dealing with how competent images-of-achievement are created. However, my attempt is to inject a small dose of reality into your pre-putt thinking. I want you to see whether you can stick with your original plan to make a good stroke and not be derailed by a last second interruption. Better to plan for the possibility of a negative thought than have it surprise you. This is rather like Tiger Woods being able to do what almost none of us can do—stopping a driver swing (at 110+ mph, I might add) in mid-stream. Teach yourself that just saying something doesn't necessarily and always make it true. Teach yourself to putt through adversity.

Putt the Tee Drill. This is more of a technique drill that's "above my pay grade" but it has merit for the analysis of putting errors. Set up to make a short straight putt using a tee, as a substitute for the ball. Putt and see what happens to the tee. If it is bent in line with hole, then the stroke was square. Any bending left or right will show you you're either pulling or pushing your stroke.

Much attention has already been directed to the importance of proper sensory and positive memory cues in the creation of putting competence and confidence. But, this is only part of the story. Direct your attention to the chart at the start of this chapter. The items on the bottom line are the four essential building blocks of self-confidence. Putting confidence certainly arises from successful putting outcomes, that's a given, but there are several other variables that must be brought into the equation if success is to be optimized. Look again at the obvious: putting confidence is gained from your putting competence—you'll be more confident if you make more putts. But what else helps you make more putts? Your capacity to <u>concentrate</u> correctly; your <u>commitment</u> to quality pre-putt preparation and deliberate practice; your <u>control</u> of images, thoughts, and emotions; and <u>consistency</u> in your preparation and putting stroke. Understanding each of these building blocks and employing strategies to enhance them will go a long way to complete the answer to the following questions: "How do I get to be a more confident putter?" "What do I need to do?" The following four chapters offer some directives.

EIGHT. CONCENTRATION

Preparing to putt is initially in large part a visual task whose demands are static and right in front of you. There's no ball coming at your head with great velocity, nobody trying to stop you from reading your putt's direction, nobody blitzing you to cause you to hurry the process, and no time clock to constrain your preparation. On the other hand, the task is difficult—golf architects and superintendents aren't your friends. There are many cues to see and many others to dismiss. This is reminiscent of the dilemma Sherlock Holmes faced in the *Adventures of the Naval Treaty* when he had to sort through the necessary and useless clues in order to discover who stole the important naval treaty: *The principal difficulty lay in the fact of there being too much evidence. What was vital was overlaid and hidden by what was irrelevant.* But, of course, his concentration skills were once again impeccable. But, that's such a good way to phrase it: too many clues and the useful ones are hidden by so many irrelevant ones. That really expresses the problem golfers have in reading greens. Where should our concentration or focus be?

Concentration, also referred to as attention, is so crucial because it is the gateway through which topnotch putting is possible. From previous reading you realize the importance of a competent plan of action; and you have always understood the importance of accurately reading breaks and the subsequent necessity of matching distance, break, and putting speed. Another thing you're way too often aware of is that breakdowns occur and putts are missed—putts that "really" shouldn't be missed. Putting is a combination of perception, conception, emotion, and physical action. It is proper concentration that puts all these together in one consolidated package or plan, one that will lead to a competent outcome. I believe most golfers approach putting without much awareness of the complexity of the task nor without enough knowledge of why and where things can go wrong.

Let's spend a little time here to highlight some of the hopeful putter's obvious pitfalls, many of them the result of either not being very attentive, being attentive to the right things at the wrong time, or simply focusing on the wrong things. Here's the litany; see how many might apply to you. Do you hear yourself saying "I didn't see that sharp break at the hole"? Why not, it was there to be seen. Is it possible that you weren't diligent enough, maybe without even realizing it? Are you too casual with your green reading process? We know that putts tend to break more when they slow down, and that's usually near the hole. Perhaps your time in pre-putt preparation is spent more on thinking about the outcome, usually not in a positive manner but more on the difficulty of the task and the limited likelihood of success. Or, as I might say, you're in your brain "muddying" up the works rather than outwardly focusing on the necessary cues. There's a time to be "out there" and a time to be "in there," but you can't be both places at once. Certainly you can and must "flip flop" your attention from external to internal as long as focus in one area doesn't interfere with another. Let me offer you an example. The assessment of the amount of break is not going smoothly, you're confounded by both the direction and degree of break (external focus). So a thought arises that confounds the read and slows the discriminating process down: "I don't see how I can even get this putt close and avoid a 3-putt" (internal focus). This does nothing but distract you and interferes with the sorting out of organizational input. And any attempt to change external and internal channels rapidly and continuously ("multitasking," so to speak) will result in system overload. Are you a channel flipper? What if I asked your life partner?

The message I want you to get is that the process of pre-putt preparation is sequential (i.e., one task at a time). Specifically, consider adopting the following order:

* Read the direction and amount of break.

* Create the feel for the putt's distance taking into account the slope.

* Add or subtract (control) your emotions; increase the urgency if you must have this putt or else, and decrease your

nervousness if it's likely to impact your touch or stroke. You'll sense the latter by the intensity of your feelings.

* Follow your routine and ritual, and initiate the putt.

What this order does is heed the advice of Richard Restak, one of the nation's leading experts on the brain (and remember putting is brain science), that we take advantage of the brain's various modes or channels of processing and select the one that best meets the task demands at any particular moment. We do this with our <u>focus</u>—paying attention, being diligent, and staying on task. Allow our input to be as <u>multisensory</u> as possible—visual, auditory, kinesthetic. And, one more necessity. Plug into your <u>memory pegs</u>, those basic rules that need to be incorporated into your plan of action (e.g., putt the ball past the hole if it misses, the greens are slower today than yesterday, putts tend to break more around the cup) BUT not things like "I'm a lousy putter" or "My last putt didn't break as I expected." The latter aren't memory pegs, these are hooks that hang you out to dry.

In putting, downtime is the golfer's enemy because there's way too much lull in the action, and this provides ample opportunities for destructive thinking. What will you do to fill your time on the green waiting for your turn to putt? All it takes is the wrong focus to sabotage your confidence. You have your mind made up, stand over the ball, and now the read doesn't look right. Now what? Go with your first impression and putt as you planned? Or, step back, reassess, adjust the plan, step in, and putt? I'm not certain I can answer this dilemma for everyone, but I have my own preference. Although I don't have any great arguments for those who advocate that your first impression is best, in fact I agree with Bob Rotella, the prominent sport psychologist to many professional golfers, that a well-planned read is likely to promote a high degree of confidence. But, here's my take on this. As you stand over a putt and you get the feeling that something is just not right, even though you went through all your pre-putt preparation keys, is it such a good idea to just go ahead and putt? I think not. Consider why the thought of missing the putt enters your consciousness. Is it just you second guessing your preparation or putting competence? Is your lack of confidence playing tricks on you? For me, at least, I welcome the opportunity to double check my read, which is usually direction not speed. If I decide my original read was correct, then I'm doubly confident in the likelihood of making a successful putt. If, on the other hand, I perceive a need to adjust the read, then I feel better that I didn't miss a putt that I had initially misread. You might recall the earlier discussion on putting the second ball first. This doesn't occur very often but I don't dismiss it when it does; it would be disastrous to your confidence if second-guessing became a habit. My self-explanation for the re-read of the putt is that sometimes my brain has a better plan of action than the one I intentionally tried to arrange. There are times to listen to your brain and times to challenge what you "hear."

When you think of concentration you visualize a golfer kneeling down behind his putt with hands cupped on the sides of his face, narrowly focusing on his target or aimline. The picture is one of single-mindedness or dogged attention to details, and perhaps only to one detail. However, when you think about all a golfer has to do to create the sensory input necessary to create a competent putting stroke, surely you'll recognize that golfers need to be able to shift back and forth from a broad to a narrow focus and also from an external to an internal focus. Let me try to make more sense of this. In reading greens, golfers need to survey the entire environment from the surrounding terrain to the way the cup is tilted (i.e., sensing everything that could even possibly effect the putt to only selecting those cues that are centrally important).

Because plans of action are created by both sensory and perceptual cues (e.g., direction the grain runs) in conjunction with conceptual cues (e.g., extracting past like putting successes from memory), the golfer's attention must of necessity switch between an external focus (e.g., "out there" in the world) to an internal focus ("in there" in your head). Perhaps a good metaphor is picturing a wall receptacle with two light switches, one labeled broad/narrow and the other external/internal. The more you can "manually" control these switches, the less "strobe effect" there will be. If these switches are on automatic pilot, then you can imagine the sensory and conceptual mess, but this is just the mess the less experienced golfer faces. One task can't get completed (e.g., reading the break) before an incorrect focus gets in the way (e.g., "This looks like a 3-putt"). No wonder the read is compromised. He or she is both inaccurate and haphazard with both sensory and conceptual inputs. Caution! This is also the mess the experienced golfer faces if and when there's inattention to precise pre-putt preparation and ritual, including a failure to add a positive bias to the image-of-achievement.

Confident putters will be more at ease and less confounded with the complexity of sensory cues. They tend to trust their green reading skills. Confident putters also have a feeling that they will achieve reasonable success (of course, this is all relative) with their upcoming putts because they tend to be able to conjure up positive images. And, I believe it's very evident that when golfers can meet the concentration demands placed on them (and certain putts demand a lot more attention than some others), their sense of putting confidence gets a real boost. Repeatedly good decision-making breeds confidence!

If I was asked to offer just one focal point that was more important than any other, my choice would be to locate the aimline using the clock face concept. This provides a degree of concreteness to the process of reading greens, a task that's usually perceived and performed in a "catch-as-catch-can" way. Do you catch my drift? There's so much to see that it's difficult to resist scanning and chunking, rather than centralizing your focus on what really matters. And what is this? First, is the slope uphill or downhill? And, second, how much does the side slope deviate from the fall line? From there it's a matter of creating the touch to match the aimline. If it only were this easy! But, once you become ordered and diligent with your attention and concentrate on those few cues that really matter, it's difficult for me to foresee anything less than enhanced putting proficiency for you.

NINE. COMMITMENT

Self-confidence does not come easily, don't expect that you can grasp it overnight. You already know how it ebbs and flows. It tends to be elusive, fickle, and very transitory. If you wish to develop "permanent" self-confidence, then you'll need to spend considerable practice time on both fundamentals and confidence putting drills. I mean a <u>concentrated</u> plan of action. Research on elite performers across many domains (e.g., music, artistic, sports) reveals the equation for success at the elite level. You'll find the conclusions more than a bit overwhelming; it takes 10,000 <u>proper</u> repetitions to form a habit and 20,000 to consolidate it. And why are old habits hard to change? Well, first of all the change "doesn't feel right." Exactly! It should <u>feel wrong</u> because it's what? A change! So one needs to accept this fact and commit to a plan of change. Bury the worn-out whining excuse: "But I've always done it this way." It won't be easy to change because habits are the result of "imprints" laid down in the brain from thousands of previous repetitions. Habits are so ingrained that you're hardly even in control of them; they tend to appear even when conditions might demand otherwise. Take the case of professional golfers with their immaculate and tightly rehearsed pre-putt preparations. They trust their reads and they trust their touch. But, what happens when conditions go way beyond the pale? In the first round of the FedEx Cup playoffs of 2012, one of the green speeds was running at 16-17 stimps, on the flat of course (12 is a normal speed for PGA tournaments, and that's faster than most greens we mortals play). You probably can guess what happened. The best putters in the universe were leaving second puts 8-12 feet long of the hole. Can you say 3-putt? Why? Simply because stimps that "outrageous" are outside their comfort zones, which is another way of saying outside their habitual plans of actions.

Moreover, there are other findings that reveal it requires 10,000 hours, NOT trials, of really committed practice <u>over a decade</u> to even have a chance of even breaking into the bottom level of the elite category. Whew! I'm not sure many of us have this degree of dedication (and many of us may not even have that much time left), but it certainly illustrates that practice in not a "one-and-done" deal. Also, the time spent in your typical pre-round warm-up is not the kind of practice that would even count. Just the other day as I was driving I heard the old Ernest Tubb song "I've got half a mind to leave you but don't have half the heart to go." The refrain echoed in my mind over and over, and I thought that this is precisely the kind of dilemma that prevents golfers from committing to the aspects of putting they possibly realize they should be working on. But, it's readily apparent that "half a mind" (hazy thoughts) coupled with "half a heart" (lukewarm effort) will never lead to anything productive. Earlier I described a number of confidence-building putting drills designed to add variety and purpose to the typical "putting balls back and forth to random holes" practice. Hopefully, you'll be able to create a systematic putting improvement plan from these drills and the drills described earlier in the chapter dealing with reading greens.

Much has already been addressed about the importance of pre-putt preparation, pre-putt routine, and pre-putt ritual but here I want to mention each as a crucial aspect of commitment. Each of these need to be developed to the point where no putt is struck until the proper sequence is performed. Look, you don't go on a trip without packing appropriately for your subsequent activities, and you don't go hunting and fail to aim your rifle or shotgun at your targets Why then would you fail to plan appropriately for ANY putt you ever struck, and why would you ever stroke a putt without a very clear plan (direction and distance) in your mind? Just consider how good it would feel to stand over a putt, trusting that "all the stars in the universe are aligned" to allow you to stroke the best possible putt. No doubts, no worries, just trust that your image-of-achievement would create the correct speed and direction to achieve your goal. Wouldn't this be an improvement over how we often feel as we stand over our putts, especially the ones we label troublesome? Trust is the ultimate feeling every golfer needs just prior to hitting any shot in golf. It seems to me that dedicated effort in planning every putt is a key ingredient in developing trust. Hopefully you agree and will decide to accept my invitation to work at your putting in a more intelligent manner, that is if you're looking for the satisfied feeling that trust affords you.

Perhaps we should consider trying to get close to the standard set by Aaron Baddeley: *I say a couple of things I attribute to becoming one of the top putters is that one, I understand what I do to putt well—I understand my keys. And then secondly, really, I believe I'm a good putter. I believe I can make every putt, and I have a good routine and a very good mental routine when I putt.* I think we all can clearly see the trust based on his pre-putt preparation that colors Aaron's attitude. In summary, then, when you choose (and it is your choice) to fully commit to your putting plan of action, with no negative baggage, you'll be free to make a confident stroke. Greater commitment leads to increased putting confidence, and enhanced putting confidence allows for the freedom to commit fully to the task. Do you see the two-way street? Putting confidence is both a cause and effect.

What kind of practice leads to putting success? Does practice in and of itself lead to success? Or, does practice make permanent— meaning poor practice consolidates errors and good practice leads to improvement? Does practice have to be perfect if success is to maximized? Many would subscribe to the latter position that errorless practice is the road to success. But, really, practice can't be perfect when you consider all the different variables that comprise competent putting. And, even if it was possible, what would be the purpose of practice if you could perform perfectly? The only kind of practice that will lead to improved putting expertise is <u>targeted, mistake-focused practice</u>. Added to this is the necessity for golfers to practice with passion and persistence. Putting this altogether, if you're serious about improving your putting, then your practice MUST have specific agendas, MUST stretch you enough so that you're bound to get out of your comfort zone and work on difficult aspects, MUST be intense, and you MUST be persistent to maintain enough optimism to identify and work through your practice putting errors. Does this sound at all like the kind of practice you do? Don't answer this question!

Before I expand on the rationale for these essential practice characteristics, I want to offer my explanation of why golf scores, yours, mine, and most others, haven't improved much beyond the level we developed many years ago. Even though equipment, instruction, and golf courses have improved tremendously over the years, average scores for all golfers remain static. This defies logic until you realize where the problem lies. The inveterate golf instructor, Albert Einstein, taking time out from his deliberations about his theory of relativity, gave us the answer years ago but we didn't pay attention! <u>Practicing putting the way you've always practiced and expecting you'd get better is INSANITY</u>! More specifically, here's the point:

*   We don't know HOW to practice, OR

*   We don't practice WHAT we know, OR

*   We don't know HOW to practice AND we don't know WHAT to practice

Practice has to be <u>deliberate</u>. Golfers must understand the various demands putting places on them and practice enough to be competent in all situations.

Back to the dissection of the essentials of putting practice. <u>Practice must be targeted</u>; just the opposite of aimless. Golfers must go to the putting green with a purpose; and we seldom do this, do we? We stride up to the green, casually throw three balls down some random distance from a miniature flag, and begin stroking putts aimlessly at the target. Is the putt a straight putt? Is it uphill or downhill? What are you trying to learn from such poor planning? Here's what you might do. Use two or three of the confidence-building drills described earlier to work on consolidating positive feelings. Or, walk off a 20- to 30-foot distance (a good round number for how far your iron shots typically leave you from the pin), and putt your three balls to get the feel for the distance—straight, uphill, and downhill, left-and right-breaking. Or, work on putts you dislike, those big breaking putts. There's no end to the specific purposes you can select. It might be useful for you to pause for a moment or two and think about the kinds of putts that trouble you. Once you have your answers, you have directions for your next practice. Just think about all the variations you face on the greens, and practice them so nothing surprises or "depresses" you when the inevitable occurs.

<u>Practice must be error-focused</u>; just the opposite of comfortable and easy. This does not mean that your intention is to make errors but more of continually reaching to do more. A good metaphor to illustrate this point is labeled *baby staggering* by Daniel Coyle. It is only through repeated trials of errors and hundreds or thousands of repeated attempts to achieve the goal of walking that a degree of competence is gained. May I remind you of the oft-repeated adage: "There's more information to be gained from our failures than from our successes." Our successes give us a warm fuzzy feeling, and success to excess often leaves us immune to constructive criticism pointed at making us better. What does the coach of an undefeated team fear? Complacency (meaning no new learning; we're as good as we're going to get). What do we know about how learning occurs and how skills are developed? Once again we must consider what brain scientists tell us. Skill is all tied up with forging faster and more accurate transmission of impulses along chains of nerve fibers, which are coated with a sheathing called myelin. That may sound more than a little strange. Myelin? However, consider this from the world of professional golf: When Sean Foley was asked why his client, Justin Rose, had improved so much, he replied "myelin." As we energize circuits by practicing our putting, making errors and correcting them, then firing the circuits again with additional trials, we are creating putting competence. So the cycle looks like this: Putt . . . make immediate awareness of an error . . . correct the error . . . putt again. Without awareness and correction of the error(s) and subsequent firing the circuits, no learning takes place. It's imperative that awareness of an error occur almost instantaneously as a putt is stroked. For instance, the quicker you can recognize, maybe even say under your breath what happened (e.g., "I never hit it hard enough"; "I opened the face at impact"; "I missed my aimline"), make the correction and putt again, the better. A good way to identify errors and remediate them is to utilize one or more of the earlier described drills. The more often the circuit is fired, the more myelin is wrapped around the nerve fibers. And, as Coyle so aptly stated: *Struggle is not an option, it's a biological requirement.*

<u>Practice must be governed by passion and persistence</u>; just the opposite of aimlessly going through the motions. Earlier I described the equation for becoming an expert in any field, namely a minimum of 10,000 hours of deliberate practice. It's not that we should measure

ourselves against this standard but it gives us some idea of the degree of commitment required to be really proficient. What's our normal response when our driving range and putting green practices go poorly? Do we decide that we're just grooving errors (i.e., practice might consolidate our errors) and so it's best to quit? This could happen without correct analysis of errors and without the capacity to make corrections. If you don't know the problem, you'll never find the solution. This is where a good golf instructor is needed. Or, if we know the solution, do we grit our teeth, re-commit ourselves even in the face of errors and the frustration they cause, and persist at the tasks? Only the latter will enhance our competence and our confidence. Dabbling in random putting is merely a waste of time! Ben Hogan told us that the secret of golfing success was in the dirt—practice, practice, practice. But, unless the dirt reveals some truths, it's safe to say you're just "playing in the sandbox."

Contrary to what some other writers claim, I agree wholeheartedly with Geoff Colvin's assertion that golfers should never get to the point where any aspect of their game gets set on automatic pilot because automaticity prevents further development of competence. Golfers who commit themselves to the aforementioned essentials that comprise "good practice" will never bottom out their learning curves because they are constantly looking to address what they don't do well (e.g., putt under pressure, two-putt from anywhere, make short putts). Most golfers seldom improve much; great performers are always improving. Why? By always doing something different in order to achieve different results. Notice how many times this refrain crops up.

As golfers, we are often surprised and quizzical when professional golfers such as Tiger Woods and Padraig Harrington, both major tournament champions, rework their golf swings for the second or third time. Why would they do this amid all their great successes? Their collective response is always the same, namely to improve on what is already good or excellent. "He who stands still gets bypassed."

Allow me to address the steps in designing deliberate putting practice.

1. Identify and prioritize what you need to work on. This shouldn't be too difficult as some things are likely obvious (e.g., miss a lot of

short putts, miss most putts low of the cup). If nothing this clear comes to mind, then notice areas where your playing partners exceed your competence (e.g., "Jerry's a good long putter—he makes far more than I do"; "Wally never misses a makeable putt"). Failing this, consider using the coding system following the steps to identify your putting patterns—something will emerge.

2. Isolate strategies and drills to practice. There are numerous drills described throughout the book from which to choose. Select the ones that fit your needs (e.g., reading greens, building confidence).

3. Plan a schedule around the availability of the putting green, and allow yourself adequate time to complete your practice.

4. Don't try to address too many things at one time (e.g., work on short putts and work on developing feel for 20-foot uphill and downhill putts). By all means choose different drills where possible to maintain your interest.

5. Expect that your motivation will wane as you stroke well-prepared putts over and over again. In fact, it will be a good thing if you get bored because then you'll get an opportunity to test your perseverance. Fight through this state by making little goals for yourself (e.g., "Just 10 more" followed upon completion by "Just 10 more"). Practicing putting to get better is an endurance contest; if you tire too quickly, little is gained.

6. Deliberate putting practice requires focused concentration, not helped at all by the constant interactions with others that normally occur on the practice green. Get the niceties over with, firmly explain your situation, and putt in as much solitude as you can orchestrate. On the other hand, if your purpose is to deal with outside distractions, then tune in to the environment and tune out when actually planning and practicing your putts.

Accurate feedback is crucial in identifying your putting weaknesses. We can't always count on our memory to give us the correct and total picture. To remediate this, I recommend you use the following coding system when you play. Let someone else keep your score and you record the number of putts taken on each hole along with the appropriate code, immediately upon leaving the green or sooner. This system will be helpful in recording your putting competence progress once you embark on a plan of deliberate practice.

S—left putt short
L—stroked putt long
R—didn't follow routine
NP—never "saw" line, path, or channel
NC—nonchalant; didn't care
H—head came up
NT—no tempo, stroke not smooth
MH—missed on high side
ML—missed on low side
AZ—all of above (JUST KIDDING!)

After reading all the essentials of deliberate practice and being duly persuaded to implement the suggestions offered, you undoubtedly can't wait to race to the practice putting green. And, for this I applaud you. Practicing just to practice fills time and gives you a sense (albeit a false one) that you're working to improve, but now you know better. Although I'd be the last person to suggest anything that would dash your hopes, I feel a deep sense of responsibility to leave you with Geoff Colvin's caveat (you know, a caution or warning):

Any adult thinking of starting a professional career in any field in which some participants begin their development as small children should first get out the calculator and face the music.

Reprinted by permission of Finkstrom Licensing International.

Remember that you need to put in a minimum of 10,000 hours of deliberate practice over a period of at least a decade to reach the bottom level of expert status. This doesn't even include the untold hours needed to break bad habits. Brain circuits, once developed, don't de-myelinate. All this means is that most of us have some finely tuned incompetent circuits just waiting to be primed. These well-worn patterns have to be overriden or bypassed if our intention is to become better putters. The good point is that you now know how to achieve greater competence, even though your goal may not approach the loftiness of the above quote.

It's easy to understand how important commitment and focused deliberate practice are to putting confidence. As one gains more confidence, from whatever sources, commitment will also come more easily. Would you expect a golfer with low expectations of putting success to spend much time on the practice green, utilizing some of the specifics outlined above. Not likely! That is, not likely until he or she understands the two-way relationships between commitment and putting confidence, and putting confidence and putting performance. Golfers who spend more quality time on their putting will be rewarded with greater confidence and success, and that's the bottom line. And guess what? We all love to do what we're good at!

TEN. CONTROL

There are two extremely important facets that golfers must learn to create and control or each will prevent optimal putting performance and even serve as a destructive force to putting success. One is the capacity to <u>create facilitative imagery</u> and the other is to <u>control and harness thoughts and emotions</u>. Images, thoughts, and emotions are part of everyone's nature, so much so that they aren't given enough attention. That's unfortunate because they can be harnessed to serve you if you only direct them. The flip side is very cruel: Either you control your images, thoughts, and emotions or they will control you. Think of the golfers you normally play with. Can you think of any of your golfing buddies who are slaves to their uncontrolled emotions? I'm betting that some names quickly pop out! Let's first look at imagery and its ramifications.

Imagery

I never really dreamed of making many putts. Maybe that's why I haven't made many. Calvin Peete, PGA golfer

Do you think so!

If I asked you what you knew about imagery, your responses would likely be very brief. You might even say that you really don't know anything. But, you knew more about it when you were growing up. Let me ask you some questions to probe your childhood memories. Did you ever feel you needed the light to be left on in your bedroom at night? Did you make a big deal of this? Why? What was going to happen in the dark that wouldn't happen in the light? Did you ever sense that a monster lived underneath your bed, and believe it so much so that if you set your foot on the floor it would be chomped off? Did you ever see "people" in your room really caused by the shadows cast by furniture, curtains blowing, etc.? Was the situation improved if you pulled the cover up over your head? Folks, we're talking about imagination here. Answer this: Was the situation "real"? Real in the sense that it grabbed your attention by pricking your thoughts and emotions. Why do children put pictures of their heroes on their bedroom walls? Just for decoration? You know it has a much greater purpose. Pictures of those individuals who have already reached a level of performance that you may have desired fueled your inspiration and put your goals in motion. How does it work? By you imaging that you were this person and/or that you wanted to achieve as much, maybe even more, than your hero. Revealing, isn't it? You knew all this but you grew up and left childhood things behind. Unfortunately you left behind an untapped source of your own power that, if harnessed, has the capacity to raise your level of performance to unknown heights.

Imagery is certainly not a new term, although its prominence has risen in the last three to four decades in golfing circles probably by the pronouncements of Jack Nicklaus in his 1974 book, *Golf My Way*. But, before we proceed much further, let's take a look at what we mean by imagery. Imagery consists of <u>visual</u>, <u>auditory</u>, and <u>kinesthetic</u> modes, all interconnected. Without understanding these various aspects, you might think that visualization and imagery are one and the same. Visualization is seeing the break, maybe even "painting" the expected ball track, and seeing the ball go in the cup—all in your mind's eye. To accentuate this scenario, imagery can be made even more powerful by hearing the putted ball fall over and make that characteristic sound when it hits the bottom of the cup. Can you resurrect this sound from memory? But, we're not finished yet because the image is incomplete without feeling the force required to stroke the putt along the line into the cup. See it . . . Hear it . . . Feel it!

Role of Imagery in Creating Performance

Two major questions will be pursued: How does imagery work? And why is imagery important? Imagery provides the internal representation of what we see, hear, and feel, it's universal, and it's not a stretch to claim that imagery is the language of the brain. And it seems to make little difference whether the images are perceptual (e.g., something actually seen) or conceptual (e.g., something we conjure up out of memory). Imagery serves as a blueprint for subsequent perceptions and actions. I wonder if you've experienced the following scenario? Have you ever noticed that once you purchase a new vehicle of a certain make and/or color, it seems that "everyone" else is now driving your same vehicle? Before your acquisition you barely noticed this vehicle but now you see it "everywhere." As I wrote this there was a Volkswagen ad on TV in which one person punches the arm of another when another VW goes by—noticing one prompts you to notice others. This shows how one outcome alters your perception of a specific segment of your world (i.e., a blueprint has been laid down). This is not just good for advertisers, it's good for the creation of good putting plans. If I've made too large a jump for you here, then consider the contagion that occurs once your first few putts of the round find their intended targets. Once putts start falling, competent plans and outcomes keep the ball rolling. You have created an expectation that all putts are going in. In brain science terms, you've positively biased the image-of-achievement.

You might even conclude from the success of previous putts that imagery seems to make outcomes "happen" before they actually occur. That doesn't really surprise us because of the knowledge gained in reading the chapter on putting and brain science. The process of any action is ready to be unfolded in its entirety before it's triggered. You plan consciously and your brain does its nonconscious or subconscious integration. And, sometimes your brain knows more than you know. I'm certain you've had the experience of making a putt in which you were certain you pushed or pulled it off your aimline. Did you really mis-hit the putt or did your experienced brain adjust your outcome-oriented process? More than just a few professional golfers talk about trying to get out of the way of their brain and allow it to create the correct direction and distance, of course with the necessary sensory input.

We all understand the intuitive truth of the following statement: "Success tends to beget more success." From what you know about how images-of-achievement and plans of action are created, are you able to explain why success breeds success? I'm optimistic you can do this. Can you explain why failure tends to mire you in further failure? Same answer, isn't it? Let's take a look into how one top-notch professional golfer turned his putting performance around. Consider, first, a couple of riddles. Which is easier: To believe in putting improvement once you see it? Or, to see it before you tend to believe it? Which seems like the more likely path to improvement? If you and I are on the same frequency, you'd assert that the former is easier but the latter is more productive. Vijay Singh is one of the best golfers in the world. He outworks everyone, he hits it a mile, but his putter has betrayed him. And, how important is putting to his overall score? So what can he do—work harder (not a possibility) or work better (always a possibility)? Frustrated with good ball striking but poor putting that led to a winless record in 35 consecutive events, in 2008 Vijay embarked on the "believe it and you'll see it" strategy. Sometimes this is called "fake it until you make it." Vijay's competitors and the golf TV audience understood the reality of Vijay's putting—inevitably he'd miss a putt most others would make and he'd take himself out of contention. Vijay openly stated that he believed he was the best putter in the world. What? In actuality he was anything but the best putter in the world but he persisted in believing differently. His positive beliefs purged his mind of much bad putting outcome memories. Here's the rest of the story. Vijay turned his putting around and won the 2008 FedEx Cup. The morale of the story . . . Believe in something enough and you'll be able to see positive outcomes that will enhance the probability of better performance (but let's never minimize the hard deliberate practice). Here's another truism: You'll only see things that fit your belief system. Believe you're a bad putter and you and your brain will find ways to make your belief come true.

Characteristics of Imagery

You've undoubtedly heard the old saying: "If anything is worth doing, it's worth doing well." In the case of imagery, imagery is going to be maximally effective if it's done correctly. Merely seeing, hearing, or feeling something doesn't put you on the path to expertise. Imagery needs to be <u>vivid</u>, <u>multi-sensory</u>, <u>controllable</u>, <u>action-oriented</u>, and <u>positive</u>. Competent plans of action require clear sensory input not hazy "pictures" of target lines nor rough guestimates of forces necessary to stroke the ball to the hole. That's why you see professional golfers spend quality time behind the ball developing clarity of purpose. Imagery needs to be multi-sensory to include visual, auditory, and kinesthetic cues. Recall from your earlier reading that anything you can do to bias the image-of-achievement is warranted, therefore it seems only wise to include all the ingredients you can to generate the best possible putting plan. Why do some come closer to realizing their dreams than others? Where does imagery fit in to the likes of the Jack Nicklauses, Tiger Woods, Michael Jordans, Sam Waltons, and most all high achievers? Each dreamed great dreams and wouldn't be dissuaded from their goals. Essentially, they controlled their imagery. Seeing something without believing is like not seeing it at all. For imagery to make an impression on the brain it must take root. Conceptual images (e.g., thoughts of who you want to be and what you want to become) can be held onto longer than perceptual images (e.g., the amount of time you can hold a visual image before it decays), but it seems inarguable that maximizing the hold time is smart. Because the image-of-achievement is outcome-oriented (i.e., it always bring an action to conclusion), the more imagery inputs ought to be outcome-oriented. Meaning? Whether it be visual, auditory, or kinesthetic, let the end result of the image be your achieved goal. Let's say you are a "spot" putter, in which your intention is to roll the ball over a spot 1-2 inches in front of the ball. As you plan your putt, pick out the spot but shift your eyes all the way down the into the hole; then return to the ball and refocus on the spot just prior to putting.

The last characteristic of good imaging should seem obvious to you. Make your images positive even though it is sometimes easier said than done. It's akin to telling the drowning person to stay calm and stop flailing his arms. It might be helpful to make you aware of just how powerful negative images are, perhaps even more powerful than positive images. To many people negativism seems more prevalent than positivism. We tend to be nitpickers, self-critics, and perfectionists. Consider if any of the following outcomes based of negative imagery apply to you?

1. Negative imagery magnifies the time for pre-putt preparation because it has to be dealt with. Once it occurs it takes take to erase it if this is even possible, or one needs to mask it by more appropriate imagery. This takes time away from concentrating on more relevant aspects of pre-putt preparation. There's time to be external with your focus and there's time to be internal. But, when you're forced to hurry because time is running out, what are the chances for a successful putt.

How does one maintain confidence when one is conflicted about the break of the putt and how firmly to stroke the putt, and still have to deal with negativity?

2. Negative imagery disrupts and derails, even sometimes paralyzes. Did you ever look at a putt and have difficulty deciding which way it breaks? From one side it looks one way and from another it gives a different read? You're left with the great unknown, and how confident do you feel? What's your outcome imagery? The problem is you must putt without any sense that you'll make it. What's the solution? The only solution that makes any sense is to make a decision, convince yourself it's correct, trust your read, and putt. At least you have a 50:50 chance of being successful, and that's a lot better than "shooting a rifle in the air and hoping you hit your target" (metaphorically speaking, of course). Or, you could ask your playing partners if you could pass on this putt because it really confuses you. If your partners are as thoughtful and as feeling as mine, I'm sure you'll get a positive response!

3. Negative imagery engenders emotional upheaval, not dissimilar to the feelings following sharp criticism. When thoughts and emotions collide, emotions ALWAYS carry the day. The result is a loss of control of any intended preparation, which tends to disrupt a fine motor act like putting. I think you can appreciate what the combination of a nonconfident read interacting with negative memory experiences (i.e., past misses) does to any ensuing putt. The next time you hear yourself exclaim "Don't pull this putt," you'll recognize that you're about to suffer negative consequences unless you're able to overcome. What would it take for a golfer to assert confidently "Get behind me Satan"? It takes faith in your well practiced pre-putt preparation and putting routine. It's amazing how many ills are remedied by systematic planning!

Imagery Strategies and Drills

Modeling: When someone reaches the pinnacle of success in any endeavor that captures one's own particular individual's eye, then what Coyle has referred to as a *vision of the ideal future self* is laid down. This goes beyond the superficial hero worship that most individuals have, to other hopefuls who model their entire persona after their models. We've seen this recently among the professional golf ranks with golfers' swings, training methods, and choice of instructors matching that of the most elite players, particularly one elite player. Not only is imitation the sincerest form of flattery, it also provides an architectural plan to build upon. Motivation is normally seen more as a fire ignited from inside, but modeling is an outside agent internalized to light the flame. When you think of it, modeling is what good instruction entails. A golf pro looks at your swing or stroke, makes a assessment, and then offers some correction. Words usually aren't good enough to allow learners to capture the essence of the correction, so a good instructor offers a few demonstrations for the learner to model. Modeling really is the key to learning. Two examples of modeling follow.

SyberVision©: A putting episode extracted from a much larger program entitled *Golf with Al Geiberger* is available for you to watch (www.youwillputtbetter.com). Allow me to explain the contents of the program, the rationale behind the program, and how to use it. There is a sequence of dozens of perfectly repeated putting strokes and outcomes, accompanied by music but no verbal instruction. There are regular speed and slow-motion sequences. There is also a sequence where highlighted points of the body demonstrate the rocking motion of the shoulders and limited use of the hands. Every putting stroke ends in a successful outcome, just as I asserted earlier that good imagery should do. *SyberVision* is a form of sensory conditioning (i.e., perfect modeling) characterized by visual distinctiveness that will capture your attention and leave you with a positive feeling (i.e., it's exciting to watch). As an aside, I had the good fortune to collaborate with *SyberVision* in 1980 and view things up close and personal. After 30 years I still have vivid memories of my experience working the *SyberVision* display booth at a professional tennis tournament at the Cow Palace in San Francisco. Spectators would walk by, stop, watch the *SyberVision* tennis program (only the sport was different; the logistics are the same), and mimic the perfect serves, forehands, backhands, etc. I especially remember one spectator because he alternated between watching the tennis and returning to the booth to mimic perfect swings (with no tennis racket, only his arm) he saw. This went on and on. I mention this mainly to illustrate the captivating possibilities of perfect modeling. Set some time aside, you won't need much—maybe 15 minutes. Watch intently, but not critically, and lose yourself in the music, fluid tempo and rhythm of the stroke, and the sights and sounds of the successful outcome. See if you can place yourself in the golfer's shoes as if it's you doing the putting. After you've watched for a while try to "paint" a ball track from the ball to the hole. Once you've completed viewing the video, close your eyes and try "seeing" the putted ball follow its track into the hole and try "hearing" the characteristic noise that only a golf ball makes when it hits the bottom of the cup. Take the sights and sounds with you to the golf course when you practice and play to assist you in laying down the most competent neural blueprints of the putting action and outcome.

Seeitgolf ©: Available commercially for media players is a multisensory training tool for enhancing visualization. It was produced in collaboration with Aaron Baddeley, one of the best putters on the PGA tour. It consists of repeated sequences of putting with a painted red track from the ball to the hole. The expertly modeled putting strokes are accompanied by a haunting selection of music. Go to seeitgolf.com to see a short youtube presentation. Tracing the path of the ball to the hole provides clear cues to the brain, almost to the point of directing the brain to create the plan of action to achieve the intended outcome. Also, tracing the path allows the golfer to trust the "known" rather than merely putting into green space. Unless you are a very unique individual with the capacity to visualize still intact from childhood and one who can create and harness images to enhance your performance, then you likely share Bobby Jones comments of many decades ago: *Seeing the line is a curious thing and I'm free to confess I do not well understand it. I suppose it's one of those psychological phases of golf.* Well, Mr. Jones could be excused for his lack of understanding, even though he recognized the issue. But, modern day golfers are privy to so much material on the psychology of putting and my hopes are that I'll be able to convince you in these few pages to integrate some mental training into your putting repertoire.

The following three strategies are ones you can create yourself to add positivity to your plans of action and to allow for the smooth and positive execution of your putting strokes.

See it . . . Feel it . . . Trust it: A prominent sport psychologist friend of mine, David Cook, developed this three-part coaching strategy to assist his golf clients enhance their golfing performance. See it means to assess the putt from every dimension and then create a picture of the putt you plan to hit. Immerse yourself in the visualization; don't be casual about it. Feel it means to create and re-create the feel required to stroke the putt all the way to the hole (or 10-17 inches past if you miss). Most, but not all, professional golfers set up slightly away from the ball and make two or three practice putts (always the same number no matter the length of the putt) before they step in and putt. Trust it is the final part of the equation and most crucial because it either supports or derails the previous two steps. You can visualize the line and create the correct feel but if at the moment of truth you really don't trust the process, all is lost. And, I'll repeat here what I've intimated before: To stroke a putt without complete trust is sheer folly! As you stand over your putt, just repeat to yourself: See it . . Feel it . . Trust it. Seeing the outcome, feeling the stroke, and trusting yourself won't necessarily make you a star putter, but failing to implement the three-part strategy may doom you to be less than you're capable of achieving—no matter your skill level.

Recall past successes: When we dream, we create visual images, don't we? The same as when we daydream. One of the ways of bringing confident feelings to the surface is recalling past putting successes, remembering them as if they just occurred. If I could be granted some latitude here, I'd like to share an experience that occurred to me a couple of decades ago when my foursome was playing in the New York State American Cancer Society Championship. It was a rainy summer day not terribly conducive to good scoring. The course had a lot of huge undulating greens (you know, the elephant mound variety) that defied putting success. On this day, however, I made two very long curling putts, putts that you'd almost never make in a lifetime. I was excited, my teammates were ecstatic (probably also surprised), and our regional Cancer Society representative kept following us to partake in the emotion. He referred to these long putts as 'lobsters." Until the last two teams on the course posted higher scores, it looked like we were going to have an appointment in Doral at the Blue Monster for a place in the national championship. I don't relate this story to impress you with my putting prowess because this was a special day. Here's the point: The confidence I gained from this experience stayed with me for an <u>entire year</u> until it eventually wore off. During this period I expected to make every putt I looked at and was genuinely surprised when I missed. What's perhaps even more mystical is that my frequent and inevitable misses did nothing to derail my confidence for subsequent putts. It was a sad day when the bulletproof feeling left and I returned to grind it out like most other golfers. Have you had great putting days? Do you ever sit back and replay your successes? Or, are your bad misses more indelibly imprinted in your memory? My suggestion is that you take some time to return to those highlight moments and try to keep them front and center. Trust comes from a sense that you can make the putt, or at least make the stroke that gives the putt a chance to go in. When you get into this positive mindset, perhaps you'll parallel the feelings expressed in the following quote:

> *I can't exactly describe it, but as I looked at the putt, the hole looked as big as a wash tub. I suddenly became convinced I couldn't miss. All I tried to do was keep the sensation by not questioning it.* Jack Fleck, on describing his final putt to win the 1955 U.S. Open

Reprinted from http://www.punpic.hu. Author unknown.

Be the ball: No serious discussion of imagery as it relates to putting would ever be complete without making reference to the classic psychological theory espoused by Chevy Chase's character, Ty Webb, in *Caddyshack*: *There's a force in the universe that makes things happen. All you have to do is get in touch with it, stop thinking, let things happen, and be the ball.* Be the ball? Have I lost my mind? Nobody in their right mind (or left) would give any credence to this now-famous humorous bit of fluff, would they? I wouldn't have thought so until I read pro golfer Stewart Cink's comments about burying his head in the ball and only thinking about starting the putt on the right line. Is there more truth here than at first meets the eye? Two points stand out to me and they're included in the following statement. When you're standing over a putt, it's time to trust and shut down the thinking. At the most, you might allow yourself one thought that encompasses your intent (e.g., "Tempo"). All the preparation must be completed prior to making the stroke. Any last second image, thought, or feeling is going to introduce novelty into the plan of action and ultimately disrupt intention. So, *Caddyshack* reigns supreme—"Be the ball."

It's one thing to be persuaded that imagery is an essential ingredient in the creation of proficient putting performance, it's quite another to understand how to put theory into practice. It has been my purpose throughout the book to provide exercises and drills to allow the converted to build putting improvement programs that will guarantee positive changes. Following are a number of visualization exercises for your consideration.

Putting Track Drill. Choose a straight 5-foot putt. Create a putting channel with two irons or shafts. Practice putting and watch the ball travel along its path to the hole. Try to visualize a putting track. Repeat this drill over and over. Really focus intently on creating the visualized path. Don't get discouraged if you can't see the track right away.

String Drill. Geoff Mangum suggests you actually create a putting line by elevating a string attached to two steak skewers. Place one skewer behind the ball and the other behind the hole, and stroke straight putts along the line. After several putts remove the string and see if you can see the line. Repeat over and over.

Tape on Carpet Drill. Apply a strip of blue painter's tape to a low nap carpet. Place thin coasters that bars and restaurants use under beverages at either end of the tape. Practice putting back and forth along the line. This should help you begin to visualize a putting line or track. Caution: Do not use tape that will leave an adhesive residue. I absolve myself of all liability if you choose duct or adhesive tape.

Paint the Line Drill. Choose a 10-20 foot putt with some perceptible side slope. Go through your green reading process and step in to putt. But instead of putting, look up from the ball to the hole and try to paint a line (choose red or white) that represents your read. Don't expect immediate results. Repeat the process over and over. Step back from the putt and make the practice stroke that matches the stroke needed to get the ball slightly past the hole. As your practice stroke is completed, trace the intended path of the ball to the hole. Repeat over and over. Adam Scott, top professional golfer, claims that this drill gives him a really good feel for how hard to stroke the putt. Again, don't be concerned it you can't paint a line.

Phony Hole Drill. This drill is useful to teach yourself to select a different target than the actual hole on uphill and downhill putts. Decide where the target should be (either short of the hole on downhill putts and beyond the hole on uphill putts). Place a thin bar or restaurant coaster on your phony target and attempt to stroke the ball this distance. Note your progress and adjust the coaster appropriately. After several practice attempts discard the coaster and substitute it with a ball marker. After several more attempts find a mark on the green to use as a target, putt to the spot. Pay particular attention to the characteristics of the green because this will influence your decision-making on other greens. I would suggest you first get the feel of what a 10-and 20-foot putt feels like before you move to similar distances on slopes. Your mind will develop some sensory "intelligence" to draw on in the future.

I must confess that I used to be able to see putting lines better when I was playing a lot. In fact, I used to act like a dictator when my best-ball tournament partner and I disagreed on a putting line. If I could see the line, and I didn't always see it, I would do everything in my power to override my partner's read (and he was a good putter) if necessary. When I got animated, it was time to listen because of our past successes. I think you can see that putting would be much easier if perfect putting tracks were laid down for us. But, realize that there are <u>many</u> perfect tracks depending on how firmly you plan to strike your putt. Professional golfers may choose to bang short putts into the hole to eliminate the break, whereas you may choose to stroke the ball to the front edge and allow it to break into the hole. Seeing, feeling, and trusting is a personal matter that no one can give us—it must be earned.

Thoughts and Emotions

Your beliefs become your thoughts
Your thoughts become your words
Your words become your actions
Your actions become your habits
Your habits become your values
Your values become your destiny
Mahatma Gandhi

Just STOP reading . . . sit back and stare off into space. Just stop and do this . . . before you continue reading. Now, what thoughts came into your head? Did you consciously plan these thoughts? Did you have many thoughts, or was there one central theme? What caused these thoughts if you didn't plan them? Were the thoughts related to what you've been reading or were they "off the wall" thoughts? Here's the point of all this chatter. You will generate thoughts from birth until death, and that's fine because that means you're alive. What isn't always so fine is that your unconscious or subconscious brain will generate any number of thoughts even though you aren't intentionally directing your thought processes—almost like unwanted advice ("I don't need to hear this"). The bottom line message to be gained from this is that you have a choice when you're planning any action, putting or otherwise, of orchestrating the content of your thoughts or "allowing" your thoughts to simply bubble up from your unconscious. Who's in charge? Would you rather hear "I feel I can make this putt" or "It looks like a 3-putt to me"?

It's obvious that thoughts cause actions, but you might wonder how something so airy and formless as a thought could impact something so concrete as a putting stroke. In the above quote, we read that thoughts become words, actually self-talk, and words become actions. Does merely saying something make it so? When you consider the role of sensory and conceptual images (seeing, hearing, feeling) in the creation of images-of-achievement, I believe you'll see how an ill-advised intentional or unintentional comment can throw a monkey wrench into your planning and subsequent performance. This leads to the obvious conclusion that you must control your inner dialog.

Thoughts also trigger emotions, and likewise emotions trigger thoughts. It's difficult to separate the two. If you allow a thought such as "I can't make short putts" to percolate upward from the depths of your memory banks, then what kind of emotion immediately follows? Does doubt, uncertainty, anxiety, panic, or fear ring a bell? Let's call thoughts and emotions co-variants because of their close interrelatedness. As one goes, so goes the other. But, for the purpose of gaining a better understanding of the two terms I've decided to deal with them separately with the proviso that you realize their commonality.

Situations that Require Control

Certain putting situations seem quite naturally to provoke <u>doubt and uncertainty</u>. Some of the more obvious situations are long breaking putts, putts that really mean something special, unfavorite putts, and others you can list. Uncertainty is bound to lead to a questioning of your putting competence and a lowering of your putting confidence. The negative thoughts are bound to flow like an entire squadron of gnats. You can't putt with this mess rolling around in your head, disrupting your plans if you've even been able to quiet things enough to strategize. What steps can you take to gain control? First, you need to shut down the inner dialog—"SHUT UP!" Second, you need to focus intently on your pre-putt preparation (See it . . . Feel it . . . Trust it) and less on outcome. Certainly you want to make the putt, but I encourage you to focus on the process because it's the thought of the outcome that bothers you. Does this make sense? And, remember you can control everything until the putted ball leaves the putter and then outside factors take over. Really, you don't make or miss the putt, you only make the stroke. The outcome is clearly another matter. Can you understand and come to grips with the subtlety here?

Perhaps you can appreciate that you already practice this narrowing of attention in other situations. Have you ever had the experience of driving a car in heavy traffic and needing to locate an unaccustomed turn? When the radio is blaring, what do you do? When your passengers are talking back and forth, what is your request? You need to focus narrowly on the task at hand or your performance will be hampered so you quiet things down. Intuitively you know this. Well, then, take this knowledge to the putting green. Third, you need to move away from doom thinking to thinking what a great achievement it will be if and when the putt goes in. What kind of putts excite you the most when they go in? Have you never seen the Tiger Woods' fist pump? You play golf for the few great shots that will bring you back the next day. Here's just such an opportunity—embrace it! Fourth and last, you need to step into your putt (See it . . . Feel it . . . Trust it) and kick start your putt with your ritual.

With the exception of short putts, golfers miss more putts than they make, and this fact doesn't go unnoticed by our brains. This tends to result in a greater likelihood of our putting plans having a negative predisposition, depending on our level of putting competence and confidence. On greens negative thoughts abound and take the form of negative self-talk. You might recognize yourself in the following admonitions: "You loser"; "Why do I play this game?"; "I just can't putt"; "I've got to be the worst putter who ever played"; "If I could putt I could play this game"; and on and on. My apologies if I missed your favorite self put-down. Everybody talks negatively to themselves, some more than others, and some way more colorfully than others. Those among us who border on being wise recognize our negative dialogs, and the real intelligent among us challenge the veracity of such negative verbalizations, but maybe none of us to the degree of Scott Peck:

> *Somehow, by Her grace, I knew that God didn't consider me* [insert your favorite put-down here— Peck's was very colorfully off-color]. *Then what was I*

doing leveling such epithets at myself? Was I smarter than God? That smacked of arrogance. I realized that God had no expectation that I should be a perfect golfer—or a perfect anything—and since She was quite willing to forgive me my imperfection at the game, I might have a certain obligation to do the same. Only my pride stood in the way [and it's said that pride goeth before the fall; Peck chose to make God female].

It's rather strange how we'll accept the negative barbs we throw at ourselves when we'd bristle if anyone else directed similar negative comments our way. I wonder why that this? Clearly we're not all masochists. I guess we hear it so often that we take it for granted, and we can get used to most anything. After all it's just idle chatter, isn't it? Let's say you believe I might be able to help you with your putting so you hire me as your mental coach. What would you do if I watched you putt and labeled you with the name(s) you call yourself (e.g., "You dumb SOB, how many times do I have to tell you . . . ."? Would I still have the job? And what impact would my coaching comments have on your putting performance if I was continually negative and sarcastic? You'd fire me on the spot, and your reactions to my comments would take one of two directions. Either you'd be so irritated and angry that I talked to you this way or, if you respected my reputation as a great putting coach, you're putting confidence would be shattered (unless I balanced my comments with some positives). BIG question: What makes you think your own personal self-created and self-directed remarks are all right, whereas my remarks are unacceptable and hurtful? Stop and ponder this question for a moment. I can only hope that your eyes widened and you exclaimed "WOW." The idea that you accept self-criticism and reject others' criticism must be challenged. Do you think that most successful golfers hear the degree of self-criticism you hear? Do you think they were born with immunity to the self-criticism gene? Or, is it more likely that they use self-criticism to motivate themselves to practice harder and better and to place a damper on negative self-talk during competition? In the vernacular of today, "asked and answered." If you'd allow me to be candid here: Constantly listening to and processing a constant dialog of escalating negative crap is just plain STUPID! Sorry, my apologies. Mea culpa. My bad.

Could controlling your thoughts really improve your putting performance? Vijay Singh certainly thought so because he worked himself out of putting mediocrity by going public with positive self-talk. Even though his published affirmations that he was one of the best putters in the world raised eyebrows because his key misses had become legendary, he persisted on his path to success. If you know anything about Vijay, you know nobody works harder at the game than he does. Positive thoughts turned into positive beliefs, and with the addition of his work ethic look what happened. Vijay became a better putter because his putting confidence rose, and when confidence is elevated negativity declines. Vijay provides us with an excellent model of success, one we all could benefit from imitating.

Perhaps you might recall an earlier quote from David Duval that golfers must do everything to protect their self-confidence. Let's apply that assertion to our discussion here as we often get emotional, sometimes out-of-control emotional, when we miss putts that we really had no business or expectation of missing. Can you put yourself in this situation? Do you have in your golfing experience the memory of a missed short putt that cost you something—something important? Not to the degree of a missed putt to lose the Masters. If so, can you resurrect and describe your thoughts, your self-taking or self-labeling, and your emotional state. How could you miss such a putt? What memory traces are you leaving in your putting repository? Nothing good, you'll hopefully agree. So, do what the best golfers in the world do. They make excuses, move one hand to the side to show everybody (but more importantly themselves) that the putt "should" have broken in that direction or "should" not have broken. It's as if the laws of gravity were suspended for them in that tiny microcosm of time and old truths no longer applied. "Come on" you say! The point is this: Taking responsibility for every small failure at one small point in time has the capacity of chipping away at what is sometimes the fragile veneer of putting competence and/or confidence. And, as long as you recognize your need for greater attention or more practice, or whatever was the real reason for the missed putt, and commit to address the issue, this isn't a problem. If you can do this, then you aren't developing a nasty character flaw. And I think you know where character flaws eventually bite you.

You can't change yesterday but you can change today's and tomorrow's outlook. If you find yourself dwelling on the past, then this is something you need to address. All our past putting attempts are represented in memory, and I've stated earlier that the negative storage is larger than the positive storage. Which memory would you choose to draw from if you had a choice? It is your choice, either by omission or commission of intent. Here's what I mean. If you let your putting plans of action develop without intentional control, then you're not in charge of the process. Only if you take charge can action be biased by positive thoughts and rosy outcomes. Perhaps putting without positive preparation and intention is like playing roulette and placing all your money on red #3 hoping you'll succeed against all other numbers and colors. Sounds a lot like Russian Roulette to me.

Perhaps nobody has "cut to the chase" more succinctly and accurately than Bob Rotella in his book *Putting Out of Your Mind* when he asserted the following: *Thinking the way you have always thought will almost certainly assure that you will putt the way you have always putted.*

Doesn't this remind you of Einstein's definition of insanity?

So, you read this book in the hope that it would offer you some methods of improving your putting. You see from the above quote that your thinking MUST change for your putting to improve. Hopefully you'll find enough substance in one or more of the following strategies that you'll be motivated to test out their validity FOR YOU. I know they work; it's your task to personalize them if you're serious about change.

<u>Strategies to Control Thoughts</u>

I wrote this book for the sole purpose of convincing you that will be a better putter when you understand more about the putting process and utilize some of the described strategies and drills. I tend to believe that you chose to read this book because you expected that its contents would deliver on its promise to improve your putting. To further this end the following strategies to control negative thinking are offered. Because we are constantly filled with thoughts, the first step to stopping negative thoughts is to recognize them the moment they appear.

Thought Stopping. Negative thoughts can start rather innocuously (e.g., "This putt looks tough"), increase in power (e.g., "I hope I can get it close"), and ultimately morph into hopelessness (e.g., "This is a guaranteed 3-putt"). Notice how an innocent comment turned into a equation for failure. It would be great if we all had Dave Stockton's attitude that he never thought there was a putt he couldn't make. Because we don't, we have to stop the negative thoughts from coloring our perceptions. Here are several options for you to experiment with:

* Recognize the thought, grit your teeth, and yell STOP or SHUT UP as loudly as you can with your inside voice or just slightly under your breath. When you're at home or alone, yell out loud. Seriously, practice this and see whether you can stop a thought and notice how long before it reappears.

* Visualize a bright red STOP sign, better yet one with a blinking red light on top. When you recognize a negative thought, trigger the image of the STOP sign.

* Wear a rubber band around your wrist. When you recognize a negative thought, snap the rubber band and I can guarantee that the sharp sting will change your thoughts. The sting is just momentary but clearly a great way to interrupt a thought.

Thoughts tend to recur so once a negative thought is stopped it MUST be replaced immediately by a positive thought. Look back at the three negative thoughts that ranged from innocent to disastrous mentioned above. After these thoughts are recognized and stopped, they could be replaced by "I've made putts tougher than this one"; "My intention is to make every putt"; and "I can handle this one." You can develop a whole array of personal positive thoughts that you can instantly draw from.

Narrow Your Focus. Become tunnel-visioned with your concentration. Do you remember the children's story about the little train attempting to climb the grade? "I think I can, I think I can" was the repetitive self-coaching point that led to success. This describes a narrow internal focus that doesn't permit any outlying thoughts to enter because conscious and intentional thoughts have to be dealt with sequentially (i.e., one at a time). If you hold tight to the positive thought, then you're more likely to create a better outcome. Another way of pushing negative thoughts to the background is by adopting a narrow external focus (e.g., intently trying to paint the ball track). Just like thoughts, concentration flip flops from internal to external all the time but not if you control its direction. And, when you narrow your focus on appropriate task demands, then you defuse potentially damaging thoughts.

Rational Restructuring. Negative thoughts that turn into negative self-talk must be challenged because most of the time they have little validity, but they can be disastrous. This is something that YOU have to do because you're the one doing the thinking. The best I can do is offer some examples of positive and negative thinking. What I'd really like you to do is search your memory for the negative thoughts you tend to hear repeatedly, write them down on one column, and construct a short positive challenging thought to write down in column two. Like the following:

Negative self-talk	Positive self-talk
"Nobody could get this putt close"	"I've got it read right"
"Just get it close"	"I plan to make this one"
"This looks like a 3-putt"	"It's hero time"
"Don't leave it short"	"I feel the distance"
"You loser"	"God created winners"
"I just can't putt"	"See it . . . Feel it . . . Trust it"

Now it's your turn. Do you notice that all the statements in the first column stem from a lack of trust. Remember what Jack Nicklaus said about trust? It's standing over a putt acknowledging that you've made it time and time again. Does trust ensure success? Of course not, golf offers no guarantees. Trust is a commodity that's gained through deliberate practice and precise pre-putt preparation, both physical and mental.

Give In . . . and Trust. It's inevitable that you'll find yourself in a totally unresolvable situation when you look at a putt. Does it break right? Does it break left? Does it break at all? Chances are it has some break because very few putts run dead straight. You look at the putt from different directions and you get mixed messages. When in doubt, play it straight? That's not such a good strategy if you can see it breaking both right and left. You can't give up and raise the white flag, so what do you do? A couple of ideas come to mind. Some would argue that your first read is likely more correct, so trust it and putt. You might want to play the odds and make a prediction of the break based on other putts you've seen, both currently and in the past. If you can conclude that the putt is more likely to break one way over the other, say 60:40, then go with the odds that favor the direction of the break. The one thing you want to avoid is putting tentatively because you're not sure. This approach will absolutely guarantee failure. No matter your plan, the only thing you can do is trust it; I can't emphasize this enough!

The strategies just described are useful in the planning stages of putting but my experience tells me that negative self-talking tends to be just as much, if not more, of a problem once the putting outcome has been determined. Why? Because golfers are in the midst of playing and negative thinking can bubble up and infect all subsequent parts of our game. It's often said that we can learn more from our failures than our successes. But, there's two ways to look at this adage— optimistically or pessimistically. The optimist would feel good about his success and applaud himself and yet utilize his failure as a measuring stick of his progress and what still needs to be done. The pessimist would be somewhat surprised at his success and less likely to feel gratified. But, more importantly, the pessimist's response to failure is one of self-deprecation fueled by the typical negative self-labeling. The only learning that comes from pessimistic thinking is that failure tends to feed into the negative self-fulfilling prophecy (e.g., "I'm just no #@%/* good"). Just as it's important to control your thought processes in the preparatory stages of putting, it's especially important to keep your head in the game by controlling your thoughts once a putt has been missed.

Post-putting Routine

Few golfers pay much attention, at least not systematic attention, to their post-putting analysis. It's difficult to learn from your putting outcomes if you have no solid information. I'd like you to consider the wisdom of implementing the following sequential post-putt strategy when putts are missed:

React . . . Quell emotions . . . Forgive . . . Learn . . . Reframe outcome . . . Quell emotions

That's a mouthful isn't it? Just call this the **RQFLRQ** strategy. Allow me to place some meaning behind each of the sequential steps. **React** means that attention is focused on what just happened. What's a typical reaction to a missed putt? The golfer turns away, blurts out the obvious fact that the putt was too short or too something, and then fusses over the miss. What was learned? What's likely to carry over? You need to watch the ball all the way to its target. **Quell emotions** immediately by using one of the techniques described in the next section. Emotions override thoughts every day and, until they are controlled or at least quieted, nothing can be learned to prevent future missed putts. In fact, negative emotions (e.g., anger) magnify the impact of the miss. **Forgive** means to excuse yourself for the miss because you made the best attempt you could under the circumstances. Ask yourself this question: "Would have I done anything differently if I had to putt all over again, <u>without</u> knowing what I now know"?

Hopefully you would be able to respond that "I did all I could do but I missed it—that's golf." The original meaning of forgiveness was "untying the knot." As your negative thoughts and feeling roll around in your head, untie the knot, let go, and gain control so the important next step can be executed. **Learn** why the putt missed. Watch professional golfers step back and study their target paths to try to understand why their putts didn't break as expected. Notice their demeanor. They have passed through the react, quell emotions, and forgive steps; they're still not happy but at least they have dulled their emotions to a point where rational thinking and analysis can occur **Reframe the outcome** is a way of trying to bring positive closure to the inherent negativity of a missed putt. Fortunately nobody has to teach you how to do this because you already know—you do it all the time. Let me jog your memory. Have you ever stubbed or caught your toe while walking? Automatically you look down for the raised bit of sidewalk but it's absolutely smooth ("It couldn't have been my fault"). Any softball or baseball players out there? Did you ever have a ground ball go under your glove? Automatically you look down and check the webbing of your glove to inspect the hole that . . . surprise . . . surprise . . . isn't there. Or, better yet, did you ever pick up imaginary pebbles or pebbles not even in the path of the ball? I could continue with more examples but you get the point. Why do you perform such charades? Who are you trying to fool? The world-out-there knows what happened. You do this to save face (your own "face") because the truth hurts. Are you ready to believe you're a klutz or a lousy ball player? You intuitively know that always taking personal responsibility for your outcomes tends to diminish how you feel about yourself so you invent ways to diminish the negative outcome. Even the best golfers in the world tamp down spike marks that aren't there and express complete surprise when a putt doesn't break as expected ("How could the green do this to me?"). <u>Here's the key point</u>: While it is useful to attribute outcomes to faulty equipment, imaginary objects, rub of the green (luck), and task difficulty ("Not even the best putter in the world could have made that putt") during play to maintain confidence, the intelligent golfer hurries to the putting green once the round is over to work on his mistakes. **Quell emotions** once again to attempt to purge the system of any residual negative feelings that would potentially impact future shots or putts. This would then be a good time to record the reason(s) for the missed putt, utilizing the coding system outlined earlier in the commitment chapter. Some techniques useful in stabilizing emotions as you walk off the green to the next hole are described in the next section.

It took me a long time to describe the **RQFLRQ** technique, and it took you some time to read it—and it won't be grasped without several readings. However, the whole sequence can be performed very quickly. **React** takes no time, just watch the ball all the way. **Forgive** merely requires a "I did my best" self-verbalization. **Quell emotions** by utilizing a momentary stress-reducing technique. **Learn** and **Refocus** are accomplished together as you offer plausible reasons why the putt missed. **Quell emotions** is done as you depart the green and can continue until you reach the next hole. So, just remember, the next time you miss a putt, **RQFLRQ**!

> *We are about as effective at stopping an emotion as we are in preventing a sneeze.* Antonio Damasio, renowned neuroscientist

Well, that rather dooms some of us, doesn't it? As golfers we understand the difficulty of getting the ball into those tiny holes in a respectable number of strokes. Sometimes the task is too harsh and the conditions "unfair" for us to achieve respectability. This leaves us unhappy, aggravated, and sometimes downright angry. Excess emotions, particularly negative emotions, have the capacity to destroy future performance along several lines. When our emotional states exceed the emotional demands of our tasks, then performance disruption occurs. I wonder how many poorly executed golf shots are caused by out-of-control emotions? The more touch and feel the shot requires, the more in control one needs to be. And, isn't touch and feel the essence of putting? At this point in your reading, I expect you have a good understanding of how any action is created. A missed putt is recorded in memory as one glitch, mistake, error—whichever label is best. Consider what happens when you wrap negative emotion around the miss and keep the miss alive by obsessing and negative thinking; much like psychological myelin wrapping. What does one miss, something even the best putters in the world do routinely, become? One miss becomes magnified many times until it reaches the point of being a calamity. One miss can actually be a round destroyer, can't it? Putting confidence and overall ball-striking confidence ride on the back of self-confidence. The golfer's positive outlook becomes unhinged by an overreaction to one missed putt. Let's be sure we understand what just one missed putt can cause if we're not vigilant and not ready to put on our psychological armor:

* histrionics (outbursts, obscenities, throwing putters)

* negative self-labeling ("I'm a loser")

* mental resignation ("quitting" because the round is over)

* failure to understand the reason(s) for the miss

* prevents closure (sets a negative attitude for all subsequent shots)

We're told we can't stop emotions, and yet some golfers react differently to their putting failures than others. Is that because they're emotionally bereft, or do they have some character strength to keep emotions intact? And, yet, some excellent golfers are more expressive than others.

Retief or Woody? Retief Goosen and Woody Austin, both successful professional golfers, seem to be at each end of the poster child for suppressing emotions and letting them out continuum. Nothing "seems" to bother Retief, although I don't have any idea of his inner churnings. Good shots, bad shots, they all get a similar response. Maybe there's a smile or two for a great shot, but never an outburst for a bad shot. Maybe he doesn't care that much—NONSENSE, he wants to win as much as anyone. Now Woody, on the other hand, lets you know exactly how he feels. We don't need any golf commentator to direct our attention to Woody's assessment of a poorly executed shot. His histrionics are legendary, but we're often prompted by the commentator to "Watch this" when Woody has to extricate himself out of a difficult situation. As an audience, we love train wrecks! Woody is unquestionably very successful and yet his emotional responses seem to undermine much of what I've said earlier about the hazards of excess negativity. This seems to beg the question: Because we can't prevent emotions, are we better off displaying or suppressing them?

If we wear our emotions on our sleeves, as they say, we increase the chances of losing control and I think you could list areas in which this would disrupt putting performance. There's a certain contagion or escalation that occurs when emotions are let loose. One's initial slight and fairly normal level of aggravation following a missed putt could ultimately result in snapping the shaft of one's putter or throwing it unless emotions are controlled. "Snappers" and "throwers" might jump into the argument to defend their actions by claiming that keeping emotions inside is too dangerous because suppression would eventually lead to an emotional explosion. Retief doesn't seem ready for a Mt. Vesuvius or Mt. Saint Helens moment anytime soon. It's not my call to judge others' behaviors, but I make it my responsibility to explain potential subsequent repercussions. It seems to come down to a cost effectiveness decision. Does expressing what most would call negative emotions help or hinder performance? Perhaps Woody Austin would say that his expressed emotionality is needed for him to play at a high level. And, as long as he's not fooling himself, "Good on ya," as his Australian playing partners might exclaim.

For most of us, there is usually a cost of expressing emotions. If we're in agreement on this, then it behooves us to get a handle on our emotions. First, you must be convinced that excessive emotional displays can be harmful—convinced enough to do something about it. Second, you need to have access to some strategies that you're convinced have merit. And, third, you must commit yourself to leaning and applying the strategies that work for you. Do you recall when Tiger Woods made his public apology about his errant behavior. He made many promises but one of them was directly related to his on-course behavior (spitting, cursing, slamming clubs on the ground, etc.). This showed disrespect for the game, he stated, and he vowed to curtail his outbursts. Although he had some relearning to do on several fronts, he would have needed to include several variations of emotional control training if he intended to keep his promises.

Social psychologists have long ago concluded that there's little support for the argument that suppressing emotions leads to a dangerous build-up. What is true is that the open expression of emotions is socially learned and expression leads to increased expression until this becomes part of your persona. Nobody fist pumps more emotionally than Tiger Woods. Nobody shows more emotional restraint than Retief Goosen. No golfer is more animated than Woody Austin. Why? The behaviors have been socially learned, whether through early learning, intentional relearning, or reinforcement.

Here's a question I asked you earlier. Did you ever have a day when putts were just grazing the hole and you got on the bogey train? After six holes, you find yourself distraught and seven strokes over par. You've already shot your handicap and the round is only one-third completed. The following is my personal scenario; you create your own if the concept appeals to you. You might be 3-over or 12-over so set your own stage. In this situation it would be safe to say that your blood pressure is up, your negative self-talker is going wild, and your emotions or butterflies can hardly find a place to land. I've had this happen more often than I'd care to count, and so have you. Perhaps this is a time when we've contemplated quitting because "what's the use." I've had success with <u>drawing the line in the sand</u>: "That's it, this has gone far enough, and I'm holding the score right here." This brash affirmation, <u>adamantly stated</u> under your breath or overtly to your playing partners if you feel like putting yourself on the line, is what I call the "give in" attitude. This is just the opposite of giving up and quitting. It's rather like saying "enough is enough—I've had it!" This isn't such a novel idea; athletes and coaches have used it forever. The team is down, the coach calls a timeout, and the message to the players is to dig in their heels on defense and stop worrying about scoring. In essence, drawing a line in the sand; the nonsense stops right now. The golfer stands alone with no coach to remind, encourage, or urge him to stop fighting to make it happen and allow proper preparation (See it . . . Feel it . . . Trust it) to create better plans of action. Fairways and greens! As you might expect, it doesn't always work but the days you hold the score to 79, 89, or 99 are days that reinforce that you're in control of how you play. The alternative to drawing a line in the sand is a score of 87, 97, or 107. I really want you to try this some day soon.

Keep this idea in the back of your mind and some day when your level of aggravation is almost over the top, pull out the "give in" strategy and test it out. You'll recognize it's time to "give in" when hear such comments as "What's the use in trying, I just don't have it today"; "If I miss one more putt, this putter gets banished to the closet"; "I should have stayed home today"; or "I think I'll quit, I've got lots of tasks to do at home." If you can conjure up your favorite "give up" utterance, then let that be your cue to "give in." You have to grit your teeth and talk harshly to yourself to get your attention. And then relax, take a few deep breaths, and demand a different way of playing, one that intently focuses on preparing to make each shot the best possible. Invoke the oft-heard cliche but absolutely necessary plan of playing one shot at a time. You'll thank me the day you resurrect your round after a very poor beginning.

Perhaps you've seen the following serenity prayer cross-stitched on a wall hanging or printed on a poster somewhere:

> *God grant me the serenity*
> *To accept the things I cannot change:*
> *Courage to change the things I can;*
> *And wisdom to know the difference.*
> Reinhold Niebuhr

Basically, the message to us is to be composed when the outcome is out of our hands, to take charge of everything we can before the outcome is determined, and to be smart enough to know what we can and cannot change. To attempt to change the outcome of a putt once the ball leaves the putter face is, on the surface, just plain nonsense but more than that, it has serious repercussions. This sounds rather calamitous and it's meant to. If you've done everything possible to "ensure" a good putting attempt—there's nothing more you could do—then the outcome is out of your hands. All well struck putts don't fall. Earlier you might recall the many ways the fairness doctrine does not apply to putting. You can get frustrated and angry, even to the point of snapping your putter shaft over your knee, but for what? What you've done is allow the impact of a missed putt to be magnified many times over in your mind. The obvious result is that your lack of emotional control has just taken a chunk out of your putting confidence because that memory will be stored and will be available for re-emergence when the next image-of-achievement is created. This negative response to nothing you could control is not a one-time thing! Look back at the serenity prayer—learn to accept the things you can't change.

I certainly don't want to pass myself off as a perfect adherer to the serenity principle (I make this apologetic self-disclosure to take the starch out of my former and current playing partners' derisive comments). Golf can be a very frustrating game, and putting even more so because it contributes so heavily to our scores. Who wouldn't be unhappy missing a putt that you can make with your eyes closed? How many chances do you get to post that great score, only to 3-putt the last green? Sure, there's frustration, disappointment, and anger inherent in our putting results. But, the cost of uncontrolled and long-lasting negative emotions is too costly. And, yes, it will take work to remediate the situation. For me personally I noticed a greater adherence to emotional control once I began to participate in a local Links Players bible study (see www.linksplayers.com for information that might interest you). Failure to control abusive language and actions displays emotional immaturity, negatively impacts your performance, and also weighs on your playing partners. Solomon addressed this very clearly and succinctly in Ecclesiastes 7:9: *Control your temper because anger labels you a fool.* Once you feel that you have a responsibility to control both your actions and contribute to the positive social climate of your entire group, your thoughts and emotions pass through a filter that most often will curtail most of the outbursts. Notice I said <u>most often!</u>

In his book, *Zen Putting*, Joe Parent described the elaborate emotional-performance cause and effect relationship. <u>Before you putt</u>, doubt, anxiety and fear create a kind of paralysis that plays itself out in poorly planned and poorly struck putts. A great example is leaving putts short when you're unsure of the read. When you doubt the outcome and fear the consequences of any putt, there is no chance that you'll make a confident stroke. Why would you? You don't know where the ball will end up. <u>After a putt is missed</u>, common emotions such as aggravation, anger, and even self-loathing ("You are so bad. Nobody in the world would have missed that putt!") are often experienced. Anger is particularly worrisome. Scott Peck calls anger the golfer's greatest enemy. Why? Anger is an out-of-control emotion that takes you out of the game until you regain control. There are many more fruitful things you could be doing than expressing your anger and then trying to get it back under control. Things like going cognitive and learning from your miss. Remember how we become more proficient? By putting ourselves in more and more difficult situations, making errors, and learning what to do better next time. All of this is lost when emotions dominate your persona. Appreciate how wise the teenage golf sensation, Danny Lee, is to recognize that he needs to work on the space between his ears: *I really get depressed if I make bogeys or doubles, so I think I've got to control the anger. Those are the kind of things I have to work on and be strong at.* Hopefully, Danny will find some aggravation and anger management strategies that work for him.

Do you have any long-term feelings of irritation, misery, or resignation when it comes to putting? Do you still harbor ill feelings and fail to accept that golf isn't fair and that putting is the most unfair of all? Be serious, why should a 6-inch putt count the same as a 250-yard tee shot? Does a bunt in baseball count the same as a home run? Persistent putting woes lead to such despair that they're difficult to deal with in a calm rational way. Ben Hogan commiserated that putting carried as much or more weight than ball striking. Sergio Garcia and Robert Allenby, two great professional golfers, have been often let down by the flat stick and their reactions show their irritation. And, why not? You hit a great iron shot and the miss a short, makeable putt. Johnny Miller got to the point where he couldn't or didn't want to deal with the outcomes of a balky, yippy putter and relegated himself to the commentator's booth. There are fewer missed putts from the announcers' platform!

Strategies to Quell Emotions

Let's accept the reality that all golfers face emotional crises at some time during a round—some mild and some monumental. Interviewed golfers always point to a key shot or putt that kept the round going or turned the round around. Also, let's agree that emotions are a natural part of all of us and that they often appear unannounced and gain strength before we're ready to deal with them. Earlier you might recall I used the metaphor of putting on armor to prevent performance mishaps. Strategies are lighter than real armor, but once practiced and utilized they serve to take on the psychological armament against excessive emotions.

Tense and Release. When you're feeling any emotional distress, especially muscle tension that might hamper fine motor performance, clench your fists as hard as you can, hold for 10 seconds, and release. Repeat as necessary. Not only will it drain some excess tension out of your muscles, it will also teach you what relaxed muscles feel like.

Relief Breathing. This is likely something you already do when you sense you're becoming overloaded with things to do. Take deep breath . . . hold it . . . exhale. Repeat a few times. Under tension-filled situations your breathing tends to become short and shallow. Deep breathing remedies this situation and provides a centering, in-control feeling—like you're back in charge. That's important because you don't want to become a slave to your feelings or emotions, especially when you can exercise control.

Time-out for Worry. Don't dismiss this technique because it sounds a little weird. Recall the assertion that emotions can't be stopped. We can attempt to control the magnitude and resultant effects of emotions but the feeling is still there. Give yourself the permission to do the worrying (really any emotion) but place a time limit on it. Here's a scenario I'm certain that most golfers face. They miss a putt they feel they should have made, and they stomp off the green in a state of heightened aggravation. It's almost as if they want to beat themselves up over their stupidity, and so they do it. Now, how does the strategy work? Really worry—I mean do it up big (e.g., "You dumb $%#*&, why don't you pack it up if that's as good as you putt"; shake your head in disgust; complain to your playing partners; let the emotional temperature gauge rise)—but the tantrum MUST cease once you approach the next tee. That's it—it's over! Then, the permission ceases and you must turn your thoughts over ENTIRELY to the preparation of the upcoming tee shot. Your focus must change from internal feeling to external information processing. The logic behind this strategy is to purge your emotion if that is your normal response to failure. Do it— do it up big time—then get over it—done—move on. You've had your pity party, now let's play.

Crumple the Last Hole. This is a variation on time-out for worry. It permits the expression of emotion but again there's a time limit. Can you picture a number from 1 to 17 written on a piece of paper? Are you able to see yourself crumpling up this piece of paper until it's just a small wad? Good! I knew you could. Now let's create a scenario in which you've just missed a putt you feel you should have made on the green corresponding to the number you selected (e.g., **6**). How would you feel? At least mildly irritated to angry, I assume. As you move off the green to the next hole, begin crumpling up the imaginary numbered sheet of paper so it's reduced to a small ball by the time you reach the next tee box. Throw it away. The sooner you can destroy the miss, the better If imaginary crumpling isn't strong enough to bleed your emotions, you might try actually writing the number on a notepad you keep in your pocket, then crumple it and discard in the next hole's trash bin.

Pre-empt the Emotion. This is a strategy that is effective in keeping negative emotions from gaining a foothold. In fact, this strategy comes as close to stopping a negative emotion as any I know. Picture that you've just stroked an 20-foot big breaking putt and half way from the hole you and everyone else can see it was a horribly poor misread or mis-hit. Instead of allowing the negativity that normally follows such ineptitude, you quizzically ask your partners: "What kept that putt out?" You smile, laughingly shake your head and your partners will chime in with some utterances like "That was a close one"; "Great read"; "Come and read my putt"; "Come over here and putt mine." The miss doesn't hurt because you make light of the outcome. Essentially, by laughing at your own failure, you defuse the situation by utilizing a self-deprecation technique. And, none of the jibes of your partners hurt because you've already opened the door for their participation. Instead of becoming an embarrassing situation, it becomes a laughable one. Try smiling or laughing off your putting failures and see how well it works for you. It works for professional golfers when they get fooled by the break, and we see the smirk on their face and the slow shake of the head—the overt acknowledgment of their "ineptitude."

Backward Masking. The elaboration and acceptance of the realities and lack of fairness of putting provide a framework from which putting outcomes can be dealt with (e.g., philosophically or thoughtfully). Golfers who internalize those concepts have a better chance of dealing with putting failures because they understand that emotional responses are not helpful. These golfers understand what they can control, and they put all their effort into preparation and post-putt interpretations, essentially backward masking emotional responses. Recall that when thoughts and emotions collide, emotions always carry the day UNLESS the focus is on making a good stroke rather than what happens once the ball starts rolling. I'm enough of a pragmatist to realize that it's better to make putts than miss them, but I believe I'm correct when I claim it's better to extract future information out of a missed putt than magnifying the miss by slobbering emotions. Assuming you're with me so far, what could you do to cause emotions to almost "catch their breath" before becoming fully expressed?

Genuinely believed assertions like "Everyone misses putts, even the pros"; "The miss only adds one stroke to the 80, 90, or 100 strokes I'm likely to make"; or "I know the percentages of making that putt" might help. So might self-searching questions like "Who am I, the best putter in the universe?"; "Is the missed putt intended to teach me something that I need to remedy?"; or "Am I good enough to get upset over missed putts?" The intent of backward masking is to put negative outcomes into perspective in order to suppress the naturally occurring negative emotional responses. Professional golfers like Retief Goosen must have ingrained such a filter to enable them to maintain their cool in emotional-laden situations. Is it possible that we could do likewise? I know it is because I play with golfers who behave like Retief (but also like Woody). And if you and I would be perfectly honest with each other, there are times when we channel Woody!

Freeze Framing. The creator of freeze framing, Lew Childre, claims: *Freeze framing is an opportunity to make on-the-spot attitude adjustments so* [a missed putt] *doesn't entrap you in an emotional roller coaster.* You might be a candidate for freeze framing if your feelings carry over to future shots and putts or if you're still stewing over a missed putt several holes later. On more than one occasion, I've harbored a bad shot for the entire round and can't wait to give it more attention by talking about it when the round is over. But, I guess that's just me, right? I better have some company out there! There are a couple of good metaphors that explain the intent of freeze framing: Stop the movie! and Stop being a ping pong ball! Can you create the images? The following four steps describe the process, some of which are part of previously described strategies:

1, Quickly recognize your feeling and call a time out—STOP! You need to disengage from the negative potential of the outcome or you'll be swept away. Would you be better off with an emotional response or a cognitive response? Which would offer you information that you might use to improve?

2. Change your focus. Step back from the missed putt and search for cues that led to the miss. Rehearse the stroke you intended to make to overlay the one that didn't work. Remember the coding chart for missed putts and the **RQFLRQ** starategy.

3. Make positive affirmations. "I don't miss putts like this"; "That's not going to happen again." Affirmations can be very powerful confidence builders because they are statements that profess your intentions. If you're the least bit skeptical about the potential power of such an apparently simplistic technique, let me dissuade you by sharing a story from the 2010 Winter Olympics. Jeret "Speedy" Peterson was in contention for a medal in the skiing aerials competition, but he knew he needed a great performance in the final round to keep his medal hopes alive. Peterson held back his "hurricane" maneuver (an original and very risky multi-flipping, multi-twisting series of gyrations) for this moment. Following the competition, Peterson shared in an interview what he had written on a piece of paper prior to the competition: *I can land the hurricane. But then I crossed out "can" and I wrote "will."* And he did it! Peterson now wears the Olympic silver medal. Might writing down your intentions for improving your putting be useful for you?

4. Try to remain cognitive, and that means not falling for every emotional response.

Although much has been directed at the negative aspects of emotion, it would be a mistake to leave you with the impression that emotion is all bad. Far from it. A certain degree of emotion is required for both learning and performance. In an earlier section, I railed against aimless practice—just putting balls with no purpose in mind. You could spend 10,000 hours on aimless practice and you'd gain very little profit from your time and effort expenditure. The opposite of aimless is being excited, motivated, and emotionally-invested. I'll leave it up to you to tell me why a friend of mine, David Cook (the sport psychologist I referenced earlier), as a teenager packed a lunch and embarked on all-day, day after day, golf practice sessions. Is that aimless practice? Of course not, only someone intent on reaching very lofty goals would invest so much of himself. Because I've opened this door, I've got to tell you the rest of David's story. He never achieved his goal of being a tour player, not because he didn't put in the time, and not because he didn't have the physical skills. David unashamedly claims that he was directed to the study of the mental side of performance fairly early in life because his performance didn't always stand up to the psychological demands of high level competition. You can be certain that his students don't miss what he didn't develop for himself during his grueling practice sessions.

Remember your school days? You've got to be in the mood to learn. This entails the awareness of the importance of the lessons (e.g., "This is a good plan"), a willingness to change ("I want to get better"), and a willingness to listen to constructive criticism without becoming emotional ("You don't know what you're talking about. This just ticks me off"), a willingness to tolerate errors and understand their importance, and the capacity to not make excuses. How many of us can say we learned all there was to learn from the teachers we had? Is there any amongst us who have taken lessons from a golf professional and soon claim that the lessons didn't work? I wonder if it was incorrect information on the part of the instructor or inadequate motivation on the part of the student? That's a question I'll let you ponder.

Learning only occurs when the brain changes! If you can recall that all action (except reflex action) is generated by an image-of-achievement and also that this active mental blueprint encompasses both sensory and conceptual images, then you shouldn't balk at accepting that brain initiatives have to become more competent before performance can improve. When you look back at the preconditions to optimal learning, you'll recall that the learning atmosphere is colored by positive emotions. There is a mood and memory correlation. The emotions you experience when you practice are going to be returned to you in subseqent plans of action. So, if putting practice is performed under ideal conditions, then the learned brain initiates a positively-oriented plan of action. But, on the other hand, if practice is replete with negative emotions (e.g., apathy, self-criticism, doubt, aggravation, etc.), then look out because future plans of action are going to be tainted by previous emotional input. Let me leave you with one guiding putting principle, whether you're practicing your putting or putting to achieve something: **Focus exclusively on the process and feel that you've done everything you could do to make the best stoke**. Even the slightest slip into wondering about the outcome can spell disaster. To reinforce this point, Stan Utley, named by *Golf Digest* as "golf's latest superstar guru" states: *It's impossible to overestimate* *how important attitude is to putting. I know for a fact that I miss putts even when I'm making a great stroke if my attitude is bad.*

Earlier I claimed that we shouldn't look at emotions as inherently harmful. But, in golf, where fine motor movements aimed at minuscule targets is the name of the game, excessive emotions tend to be disruptive. However, realize there are situations in golf that demand you rise to the occasion and match high demands with higher intensity. In key situations (and understand that's relative; what's key to you and key to a tour player preparing to putt to win a major championship is different but none the less emotionally challenging), you are most likely to be nervous—that's normal—but if you are able to channel your energy into clarity of purpose (i.e., "This is my time), then you might find yourself "willing" the ball into the hole. Can you want it too much? Most certainly! But, if it's your time and you've done due diligence in practice and pre-putt preparation, then "making" it happen is not out of the realm of possibility.

Whom among all the contemporary golfers has made more highlight reels with unbelievable fairway shots ("He has no chance of pulling this shot off") and absolutely crucial chips and putts? Whom among all these golfers has the capacity to be apparently very calm during the pre-putt planning phase and to raise his intensity to seemingly will putts into the hole ('I expected him to make the 15-foot putt to send it to extra holes"). And, whom among these golfers openly reveals his emotional level following these must-to-make. shots? Asked and answered!

I hope I've created at least a little more understanding why creating and controlling positive images, thoughts, and emotions are so crucial to optimal putting performance through increasing the confidence factor. Also, looking at putting confidence as a cause rather than an outcome allows us to "paint" positive results, think positive thoughts, and be in control of our emotions. I hope you can see the going back and forth cause and effect dynamics of this model of competence and confidence.

ELEVEN. CONSISTENCY

Think of the tasks you perform very routinely. Driving a car is a good example. You'd probably say you are a good driver and feel very confident every time you take the wheel. Why is this? Every trip you take is potentially life-threatening, yet this seldom crosses your mind. The task is quite complex, made more difficult by drinking coffee, talking on the cell phone, applying make-up, tuning the radio, or admonishing the kids in the back seat. And, yet you do all this, even as you're making subconscious adjustments to the steering wheel to stay within the lines and avoid other vehicles. The reason for your assuredness is that you've routinized the task, so much that sometimes you can even drive past your planned turn and only recognize this farther down the road. "Apparently" your mind wasn't on the total task but you performed the driving skills perfectly. Contrast all this to your attitude when you were first learning to drive. Do you recall the oversteering, sudden braking, and white knuckle grasps of the steering wheel? Did the constant coaching by your instructor foul up your concentration and make you nervous, maybe even causing you to exchange one coach for another? But, now you're the master "multitasker."

Consistency enhances self-confidence because the more often you do something, the less novelty there is. Novelty is what prevents the brain from habituating, that is getting accustomed and comfortable with a task. Frequent putting practice over a prolonged period of time is what allows golfers to get into a putting comfort zone. And, comfort spells confidence as long as the challenge of the task grabs enough of your attention. The more automatic (not in the sense of being nonconscious, but always being so systematic that you don't have to think of what you're doing) you can make your pre-putt preparation routine and ritual, the more confident you'll feel as you stand over a putt. Humans are creatures of routine with almost everything in our lives, but in competitive and achievement-oriented situations we often deviate from our plans due to poor management of the situation. Our thinking and emotions often tend to undermine our trust and, with it, our self-confidence. This reminds me of an experience I had working with a high school basketball team in a performance enhancement position. During a game I was sitting on the bench, watching "psychologically, so to speak," and I noticed "our" foul shooter make two preparatory dribbles instead of his normal three. I quickly turned to the coach and said "He's going to miss it." Almost before I got the words out, the shot clanked off the rim. Lucky guess or expected outcome because "noise" entered the plan of action?

What is the bane of all golfers? Lack of consistency. We moan about this all the time. We never know day to day who's going to show up, do we? Does it have to be this way? Is the game of golf so demanding that we can't narrow our range of performance? My argument is that the more we standardize what we can control, the greater will be our consistency. Consider the following suggestions that will allow us to standardize as much of our putting performances as possible:

* Maintain the same speed of reading every putt even if you're being pushed by the group behind you (but don't be painfully slow—"While we're young!").

* Approach the putt the same way every time, always taking stance and grip the same way.

* Sight the ball-to-cup relationship the same way (e.g., two looks and be ready to go).

* Initiate the putt with the same ritual (e.g., inhale-exhale, go).

* Implement the visualization in your preparation.

* Utilize thought and emotion control strategies, when and where needed. Have them ready.

* Expect positive outcomes.

The next time you have the opportunity to watch professional golfers prepare to putt, notice how systematically they read the green, step into their putts, take the same number of practice putts, and unhurriedly and rhythmically stroke the ball. Why do they do this? Because it gives them a nice settled feeling and a sense they can make the putt.

It seems that little else needs to be added to convince you that a consistent and routinized approach will enhance putting confidence. Perhaps this is nothing new to you. But, then, why don't you practice what you know? The reasons are many. Possibly you're not acutely aware of how divergent your approach is to each putt; you think your approach is the same, but maybe you need to reassess it. Possibly you've not committed enough time and effort to really consolidate your pre-putt decision making (order by which you read putts and prepare the break/feel equation). Possibly you sometimes take practice putts and sometimes you don't. Possibly you indiscriminately take different numbers of practice strokes. Possibly you vary the number of looks at the hole before you putt. Possibly you haven't standardized your pre-putt ritual (that which initiates the backstroke). Do any of these possibilities resonate with you? Do you label some putts as scary and impossible? Do you believe you can make each putt? And, when all putts don't go in, do you believe the next one will? Do you obsess over some missed putts?

I suppose I could create a never-ending list of questions for you to consider, but I'm sure you get the point. <u>If you desire consistency, then be consistent</u>. I realize this principle will never get me into the Psychological Hall of Fame. This, however, does not negate its wisdom. Standardization with each of the areas discussed in this and earlier chapters is needed to create the best putting comfort zone. But, what do you do? You interrupt the process by excessive attentional flip-flopping, you overthink your read, and you allow some irrational thought to rattle around in your head. This is called "getting in your own way." And, everybody who has ever heard an athlete being interviewed has been subjected to the following cliche: "I've just got to play my own game and do what I do best"; "I've just got to get out of my own way." Aaron Baddeley explains it this way: *So I just sort of try and get out of my way and let the brain figure it out, and then I try to make the putt.* The reality is that the brain is going to forge the stroke whether you're mingling in its affairs or not, because brains don't care! Whether Baddeley's nonconscious approach is as good as the more conscious approach I have proposed earlier, it's hard to argue with his putting statistics. The concept of individual differences overlays much of what know, or think we know, about human behavior. More often than not we fall back on the basic dictum: "Different strokes for different folks." But, remember, what golfers tell us they do once they're successful isn't necessarily how they arrived at their stated positions or advice. We don't tend to interview golfers until they've reach a certain level of expertise.

Recall my earlier comments about learning to drive a car and how eventually you're able to turn the control of the task over to automaticity. Driving a car and putting a golf ball are both motor skills and both demand a learning progression before a modicum of success can be realized. I suspect if you asked a person who had never driven a car nor putted a golf ball to choose the more difficult task, the choice would be driving a car. But, what would experienced golfers choose? The answer is obvious even though driving a car on the highways is always a risk. Golfers actually "die" every day on the golf course because of their putting. Amidst all the harsh realities of putting highlighted at the beginning of this book, the main reason why putting is such a difficult task is that most putts are missed, more so in practice than even during actual play, and this destroys confidence.

A few years ago I read about the pass completion statistics of Colt McCoy, then the leading Heisman Trophy candidate in mid-October, 2007. The offensive coordinator at University of Texas reported that his quarterback didn't have a single pass hit the ground during two of the last team's practices. Following each occasion, McCoy followed up his game performance with 81.2% and 90.6% pass completion rates—wins over top-ranked teams. Putters would die for such statistics. I wonder what our putting statistics are? Now that's consistency; consistency between practice and game, and consistency from game to game. Fear the golfer who has this kind of consistency.

TWELVE. BRIEF SUMMARY

We've covered a lot of material in this book, all for the purpose of trying to get you to see how and where you can improve your putting. Your task is to decide what you want to delve into with enough effort to begin to make some improvement. Ask yourself this important question: What would make the most difference in my putting? Is it being able to read greens better; and does that mean reading breaks or controlling distances, or both? Would a more systematic and consistent pre-putt routine be helpful? Would something as simple as initiating your putting stroke with some type of a ritual have value? Would it be a good idea to absolutely consolidate your success with short putts? Do you know which type of putts cause you the most trouble, and can you see some ways to gain putting competence with them? Do you need to control your negative emotions? Are you a person who hears a lot of negative self-talk? Are there any strategies that look appealing enough to you to work with to control negative thoughts and emotions? Are you convinced how very crucial putting confidence is to your performance, and do you see the areas that you could improve upon to enhance your putting confidence? And, lastly, do you have a pretty good idea on how to go about practicing the drills and strategies you might choose to maximize learning? It doesn't matter where you start, any positive change you make will begin to elevate both your putting competence and putting confidence. At the risk of being redundant, I think it might be helpful to jog your memory by reiterating some reasons for poor putting—just some friendly reminders.

Recognition of Nonconfident Putting

I think it is useful to highlight briefly some characteristics or actions of the less confident putter. Let's take an honest look to see whether any of these might apply to you. There are a couple of truths that need to be mentioned again. First, you can't expect to improve performance on any task doing it the same way you've always done it. If you want to putt better than you currently do, change is necessary. Second, the initial step to making any change in your putting is to recognize something has to change, and you need to believe in the change as well as believe you can make the change. That having been said, here are some questions to ask.

1. Do you miss a lot of short putts? Consistently more than others in your group? The success rate of putts in the 3-foot range both for amateurs and professionals is extremely high. If we can rule out poor mechanics, then what's our conclusion? Something is sabotaging the typically expected successful outcomes.

2. Is your putting stroke for short putts the same as for long putts, or does the short putt promote more of a jab that a rhythmical stroke? Is the short putt something to hurry and get out of the way? If so, you subscribe to George Duncan's philosophy. The old Scottish golfer would say: *If you're going to miss 'em, miss 'em quick.*

3. Do you tend to fiddle with the mechanical aspects of putting? For example, do you change your grip, ball position, width of stance, etc., rather than staying with a consistent approach? This will take you out of the comfort zone.

4. Do you tend to react emotionally to missed putts, particularly those that most golfers expect to make a good percentage of the time? No golfer is pleased with missed putts, unless he or she is sadistic, but emotional outbursts are signs of a lack of control. Do you control your emotional reactions to negative outcomes, or do negative outcomes control your emotional reactions? Here's a more obvious clue: If all your playing partners start to duck when you miss a putt, then it's time to make a change.

5. Is your displeasure with missed putts characterized by colorful and disparaging remarks? Remember the multiple negative impact one can create by adding excessive negativity to an otherwise normal negative outcome. <u>Let a miss only count one stoke</u>.

6. Is your darkest closet filled with putters, waiting impatiently to return from your self-imposed purgatory? Interesting, isn't it? You putt

badly and your putter gets banished. If you find yourself in the practice of recycling putters, then something's not right. Chances are very good that it's not your putter's fault that you putt badly: <u>It's not the putter in your hands, it's your head in the putter</u>.

7. Does putting drive you crazy? Are you at odds with over 40% of your total strokes? Do you often throw your hands in the air and say "What's the use?" If you 3-putt early, is it over for the day? Do you carry the heavy baggage of accumulated missed putts with you for the entire round and then rehash the disasters with your buddies following the round? If so, some self-therapy is called for.

Well that's enough self-analysis! I want to leave you with a number of important principles that should serve as a summary of the central concepts you've read.

Key Principles

1. Accept the reality that a substantial number of putts will be missed. There are many variables working against successful outcomes, some of which are out of your control. You know from earlier reading that there is a distance/success ratio, even for the best putters in the world.

2. Develop competence in reading greens and feeling distances.

3. Make the putting pre-performance task as routine as possible. Have it down so automatically that it's second nature. If not, it will disintegrate during pressure situations and the novelty will undermine your confidence.

4. Fall in love with your putter and your putting stroke. If either is not to your liking, then make a change. Putters are more important than drivers, so spend the money to get the putter with the correct feel, length, loft, grip, alignment assists, and anything else that would satisfy you. Maybe you need a burnt orange grip with the UT logo so you can capture some of McCoy's consistent statistics?

5. Focus on what you can control, namely the process of putting. If you could control the outcome, then that would be my suggestion. But, because you can't, do everything possible to make the best stroke and turn the outcome over to trust (another way of saying your brain's created image-of-achievement).

6. Practice wisely, qualitatively and quantitatively. Sure, you need thousands and thousands of practice trials but to some designated end. There's a time for fundamentals practice (e.g., green reading, playing breaks, stance, head position, etc.) and a time for confidence-enhancing practice. The former is process-oriented and the latter is outcome-oriented.

7. Putt like a kid by putting pressure on yourself (e.g., "This putt's to win the Masters."). Play putting games with others with something on the line (e.g., dimes, dollars, adult beverages, bragging rights, etc.) to test yourself under self-imposed pressure.

8. As you read your intended putting line, work on actually trying to see the line in color. Also, visualize the putt going in before you putt it and hear the distinctive sound it makes when it hits the bottom of the cup. Use the *Sybervision* putting sequence to assist you in developing some visualization expertise. Plus, there's a relatively new visualization product on the market (*seeitgolf.com*) that's designed to help you see your putting lines.

9. Create positive affirmations like Vijay Singh: "I'm the best putter on the planet." Maybe that's too far for you to go right now but you can create your own positive self-talk. Conversely, do not allow or at least challenge the negative labels (e.g., "I'm such a loser, nobody in the world would have missed that putt but me."). Listen for the derogatory dialog and shut it down. If you don't, the thought will gain strength until your only recourse is to give up, go home, and donate your clubs to charity.

10. Control your emotions. Be careful not to add to the disappointment of an unsuccessful putt by heaping more emotional negativity on the occasion. It may seem to relieve your frustration momentarily but you pay for the "false luxury" in subsequent plans

of action. Unfortunately, even excessive positive emotion does not enhance putting confidence because it promotes a loss of necessary focus and concentration for subsequent shots. I don't mean to say that you shouldn't be pleased with yourself, proud that you achieved your intended goal, but only that a calm demeanor usually works better for putting.

11. By all means, don't buy into the negative labels others place on you and your putting. There certainly seems to be some value in circumventing the negativity, even if some of it is "deserved," by adopting what Taylor and Brown have termed *illusory self-confidence*. In order to maintain a degree of confidence when your putting is less than hoped for, a dose of unrealistic optimism might be the prescription. If this sounds strange to you, let me remind you that it is used all the time by professional athletes. Here are some examples from various sports: "I'm making good contact with the baseball but it seems to find the opponents' gloves"; "I feel I'm so close to breaking into the winner's circle"; "I'm making good throws but my receivers and I don't seem to be on the same page"; and finally "I'm stroking my putts real well but they're burning the edges." These might seem like excuses and maybe they are. But, what's important is the degree to which athletes believe in their attributions. For quite a while Vijay Singh didn't putt well enough to close the deal but he kept saying that he was a good putter. I'm sure this caused a lot of raised eyebrows because his putting was, to be honest, suspect. Who had the last laugh—"Look at me now!" If you can maintain a positive attitude when times are tough, and if you work, really work, on fundamentals and confidence putting drills, you give yourself the chance of having your performance match your positive attitude.

12. Recognize that you're not the putter you could be. You are a good putter in transition, really a work-in-progress, when you implement a plan to improve. But, also recognize that you're as good as you're going to get unless you make some changes. Be honest and ask yourself if you're spending much quality time on your putting. Hopefully some of the putting drills described in this book will appeal to you and motivate you to try them out.

TEN COMMANDMENTS OF PUTTING

1. Thou shalt take no putt for granted.

2. Thou shalt intend to make every putt.

3. Thou shalt ALWAYS practice deliberatively with a specific purpose, utilizing drills with specific outcomes in mind.

4. Thou shalt understand that putting is the single most contributing factor to your golf score.

5. Thou shalt be painstakingly thorough in reading greens and visualizing ball tracks.

6. Thou shalt be prepared for irrational thought and disruptive emotions by putting on your psychological armor to maintain control.

7. Thou shalt focus on your pre-putt preparation and putting routine, NOT on the outcome.

8. Thou shalt recognize that your putting outcomes will be normally distributed; some days will be better than others.

9. Thou shalt develop and utilize a standardized unwavering pre-putt preparation and putting routine.

10. Thou shalt recognize the importance of confidence to putting success, and utilize any means available to maintain optimism.

EPILOG

Well, my golfing friends, we've come to the end of our collective journey. I have truly enjoyed the writing end and earnestly hope you've enjoyed the reading end. This may sound corny and a little "old school" but, although I don't know you, I've felt a certain kinship with you. As I asked you questions, I could almost hear your answers. As I attempted to prick your conscience, I sensed you might be reluctant to accept my "truths." That's why sometimes I stayed with a particular concept or argument longer than maybe I needed because I wanted to take my best shot. There was repetition in places and it was planned. Consolidation only comes through repetition. My apologies if you felt I overstepped my welcome in some areas or was too despotic in others—please forgive me.

I've told you that I'm most certainly not the last word on the psychology of putting, but at this point you know everything about the subject that I know. More is to be learned in the future, and there will be no dearth of sources. Hopefully I've left you enough key concepts that you'll be able to separate the useful from the less useful. Go ahead and share what you've learned with your friends so they can consider the validity of your ideas. I say "your ideas" because now they are yours, and you are free to do with them what you want (except take credit for them in publication without acknowledgment, of course).

My ultimate reward, if any is forthcoming, depends entirely on the degree to which you've considered what I've had to say and have taken some of my recommendations to heart. The degree to which you'll implement some of the drills and strategies I outlined into your putting repertoire will be my satisfaction. And, certainly not to negate the impact of the book on your own putting improvement, I'll be extremely excited if you can integrate some of the substance into your children's and grandchildren's practices.

The last thing I want to do is really accentuate the importance of putting confidence. We've spent time on four separate chapters, discussing the building blocks. I suspect that you've been able to notice the clear interrelations—each is a cause and each is an effect. So, you see there are so many ways to make positive changes—even subtle changes—in your putting performances. Even small increments can mean huge differences. Consider how close some putts come to dropping. Most days the small distance of a 1-foot distance—right, left, short, long—would make a tsunami of difference in your golf score. Do you get my point? Any improvement you can make in your approach to putting has the capacity to lead to better performance. And, can you even consider the steamroller impact on your putting if you could harness EVERYTHING you read in the book.

I was convinced at the outset of this writing project that I had some beneficial advice, drills, and strategies that would enhance every golfer's putting performance. IF and WHEN you utilize just some of the recommendations in this book, YOU WILL PUTT BETTER, I GUARANTEE IT! I want to leave you with, what Restak calls, the *golden shackles dilemma*. This is for those of you who have reserved judgment on what you read and have concluded that everything is really pretty good with your putting. Pretty good but the reality is your putting could be better. Are you willing the take the step to shake off the golden shackles of pretty good, maybe even mediocrity, and give yourself a chance at really good? You need not live with just pretty good! Greatness awaits you!

REFERENCES

Apfelbaum, J. (Ed.). 2007. *The Gigantic Book of Golf Quotations.* New York: Skyhorse.

Author unknown. 1995. *Golf: Great Thoughts on the Grand Game.* Philadelphia: Running Press.

Baddeley, A. 2008, July 24. Personal interview.

Childe, L. 1994. *Freeze-Frame: Fast Action Stress Relief: A Scientifically Proven Technique.* Emeryville, CA: Alibris.

Cohn, P. J., & Winters, R. K. *1995. The Mental Art of Putting: Using Your Mind to Putt Your Best.* South Bend, IN: Diamond Communications.

Colvin, G. 2008. *Talent Is Overrated: What Really Separates World-Class Performers from Everybody Else.* New York: Penguin.

Coyle, D. 2009. *The Talent Code: Greatness Isn't Born. It's Grown. Here's How.* New York: Random House.

Damasio, A. 1999. *The Feeling of What Happens: Body and Emotion in the Making of Consciousness.* New York: Harcourt Brace.

Harth, E. 1993. *The Creative Loop: How the Brain Makes a Mind.* Reading, MA: Addison-Wesley.

James, W. 1890. *The Principles of Psychology* (Vol. 1). New York: Dover Press.

Nicklaus, J. 1974. *Golf My Way.* New York: Simon & Schuster.

Parent, J. 2007. *Zen Putting*. New York: Penguin.

Peck, M. S. 1999. *Golf and the Spirit: Lessons for the Journey*. New York: Random House.

Pelz, D. 2000. *Dave Pelz's Putting Bible: The Complete Guide to Mastering the Green*. New York: Doubleday.

Pribram, K. H. *1977. Languages of the Brain: Experimental Paradoxes and Principles in Neuropsychology*. Monterrey, CA: Wadsworth.

Restak, R. 1995. *Brainscapes*. New York: Hyperion.

Rotella, B. 2001. *Putting Out of Your Mind*. New York: Simon & Schuster.

Taylor, S. E., & Brown, J. D. 1988. Illusion and well-being: A social psychological perspective on mental health. *Psychological Bulletin, 103*, 193-210.

Utley, S. 2006. *The Art of Putting: The Revolutionary Feel-Based System for Improving Your Score*. New York: Penguin.

Winner, E. 1996. *Gifted Children: Myths and Realities*. New York: Basic Books.